ONE WAY
to write
your personal
story

by

Ed Millis

© 2002
Ed Millis Books

ISBN 0-9718402-0-2

Edwin Graham Millis
9405 Forestridge Drive
Dallas, Texas 75238-3306

Other books by Ed:

> **High Voltage, Gunpowder and Mousetraps**,
> *or The Nearly Perfect Childhood of Ed Millis*—the story of growing
> up in Dallas on the "M" streets.

> **TI, the Transistor, and Me**, *or My Dis-integrated Circuit Through
> Texas Instruments*— the lighter side of 37 years in TI, from before the
> transistor to the 64 Meg DRAM.

All words in this book that are known to be trademarks or copyrighted have
been capitalized.

Word is a registered trademark of Microsoft Corporation.

Cover photos by Shirley Sloat
Cover art by Bev Haskin.
    (What would I do without you two?)

First Edition February 2002

Manufactured in the United States of America
By Excel Digital Press, Inc., Carrollton, Texas

Dedication

This little book is dedicated to the person with a story to tell. It doesn't matter if the story is a few anecdotes or a three-volume set, but only that there is a burning desire to set the story free. I know the feeling so well. And I dedicate this book to you, budding writers one and all, with my fondest wish that you will find the profound sense of gratification that I did on my journey into the past.

Preface

You have an idea that you might like to write a book about your life? Maybe about your childhood, or your military years, or maybe just to save a few of your favorite stories? Good for you. I have a short piece of advice for you. Do it. Don't think about it—about how hard it's going to be, or that you don't remember all the rules of grammar and punctuation, or that you can't type worth a hoot. All of those excuses are minor nuisances and are of no consequence compared to writing your story.

You have no idea how to write a book? Neither did I a few years ago. Maybe I still don't, but I've written two books about my life. The first was about growing up in Dallas and the second about my career at Texas Instruments. Writing those two little volumes has been the highlight of my later life. And the same will be true for you—it will be an unbelievably rewarding and entertaining journey.

If you write a book about your life experiences, whatever they may have been, your children, relatives, friends and strangers alike will love you for it. You will have put down on paper, for all to see and enjoy, the story of life from a time gone by. It will be your personal piece of history. Yours and yours alone. No one else could have done it, but many will enjoy it.

Exactly *how* you write your book is not nearly as important as just *writing* it. But maybe I can make it easier for you to gather and organize your thoughts and get them on paper. And I have some ideas for getting it printed and bound. Others can also help you with editing, or typing, and preparing it for the printer. As I said, that's the easy part—getting your raw story on paper is the main thing, in whatever form. We're not shooting for the Pulitzer Prize here. Your goal is just to get the fascinating story of your life on paper for the coming generations to marvel over. And they will, I guarantee.

Now, turn on your computer, or sharpen your pencil, and get with it. Fear not; it's going to be the ride of your life.

Acknowledgments

As ever, dear friend Shirley Sloat did what she could to save me from public embarrassment with her red pencil and rolling of eyes. But I'm learning. There was less bleeding on the pages this time. Thank you, my dear!

Bev Haskin, my darling talented daughter, gets kudos for doing the splendid cover design and sneaking in a few licks with *her* red pencil. What a clever girl!

And let me say that I've been truly blessed by my several friends who have written, or begun writing, their memoirs, and have let me glimpse their works in progress. Thanks for sharing your babies with me. One of these friends, Jeff Campbell, also went above and beyond with a lengthy and thoughtful critique of the early scribblings of this book, much to its betterment.

Contents

Chapter 1 – one thing leads to another

I retired from Texas Instruments in March of 1989 and not a minute too soon. I had achieved my penultimate burnout after an altogether excellent and rewarding 37-year career in engineering. But I was burned out, as they say, and my "retirement speech" (which was an allotted minute before my peers, a whole roomful of whom were also retiring) ended with, "I've had thirty-four wonderful years at TI, and thirty-four out of thirty-seven ain't bad…"

Cleaning out my desk didn't take long. I had two boxes of file folders, a carton of miscellaneous tools and instruments, and a couple of armloads of technical books and catalogs. And of course, the ever-present Escher calendar, 1989 edition, and my long-suffering *dieffenbachia* went home with me, too.

This may not seem like much to show for 37+ years with the same company, but in addition I took home something I didn't realize at the time—a brain stuffed full of great stories about working in an extraordinary company at a fortuitous time. It was the goal of Pat Haggerty, early TI president and later Chairman of the Board, for TI to grow from "a good, small company, to a good, big company." It was better than that. I saw it grow from a good, small company to a good, huge company.

It was just plain luck that brought me to the door of Geophysical Service, Inc., soon to become Texas Instruments, in August of 1950. But it wasn't luck that caused me to stay with them for nearly my entire engineering career. I witnessed and participated in the birth and growth of a world-changing power from the inside. It was a unique time and place.

Since I was not really ready to retire into my easy chair, I came back into TI as a part-time consultant, and became the manager and only worker in the TI Artifacts Program, part of the TI Archives. It was a perfect job for me, a born collector, to gather and catalog TI "things," especially since I had built some of them and could recognize most of the others.

Working with the TI past, as it were, kept me in the "old days" and stimulated memories of my early career. I began thinking about all the neat and funny things that happened to me, or around me, or because of me, while I worked at TI. Many of the stories that I liked so well had become TI "lore" and were common knowledge. Others were more personal and still others not suitable to be put down on paper.

It occurred to me that it would be a shame to lose these memories—the memories of the hectic beginnings and tumultuous growth of a dynamic company—as they would surely fade away. So, after fretting about this for a couple of years, I decided to take action and unilaterally commissioned myself as a one-man-band story collector and keeper. Why? Because these were stories about TI that people were amused by, and amazed by, and horrified by. It was a back-door history of Texas Instruments that needed to be preserved.

So I sat down to write up these stories, and I could only remember about three. It was kind of like telling the comedian to say something funny. When I sat down to do it, I couldn't remember the stories. And why not? Because that's the way the memory works, or doesn't work, to be more precise. But the next day while I was driving to work, I thought of a really funny incident. Now why couldn't I think of that yesterday when I had my pen in hand? Because *that's* the way the memory works. When you least expect it—like something has tripped a trigger in your brain—up comes a recollection. Maybe it was an idle train of thought, or a word on a billboard, or something someone said. Who knows? Any time, day or night, a story from "the good old days" can come flooding back. And I will add, as you also know, it will un-flood just as quickly. It *must* be captured when it passes through your consciousness, because it won't be there long, especially if you're in the middle of something else. You *must* take time to make a note of it if you're serious about writing a book. But it doesn't take much of a note to remind you of a story—just a couple of words will bring it back for recall at a more convenient time. Although, I'll have to admit, I never did remember what "Midland/Lubbock mix-up" meant.

To properly collect stories and incidents from the past, you should set up a trapping mechanism for fleeting thoughts. Simple as that. You need to have the means to capture a thought, at any time and anywhere. And more important, you need to develop a mind-set that gets you to operate the trapping mechanism. Write a note, speak a few words to a recorder, or write it in the dust on your dashboard. Remember, you've just been illuminated by a worthwhile thought, and it may not pass your way again.

I bought a battery tape recorder and began carrying it in my car. Whenever an Official TI Fleeting Memory would surface in my brain, I would fumble around with the recorder buttons and the mike, kind of a predecessor to the cell phone driving hazard of today, and speak a few words or a sentence or two into the recorder. It didn't need to be much to re-trigger the thought when I got around to transcribing it into the computer. I had already found out that, "Oh, I'll remember that!" didn't work. I couldn't count on remembering anything that passed through my mind, particularly after two minutes on the Dallas LBJ Freeway at rush hour. I also carried a small note pad in my shirt pocket, just in case I had an enlightening flash when I wasn't in my car. A word or two jotted down was sufficient.

Being an engineer, I had to over-organize this effort and put it in the computer. I used a DOS database program called pfs:FILE, at the time touted to be the latest and greatest, to collect my "incidents." I generated a form to fill out for each story. The form, as shown below with the headings in bold-faced type, was long and ponderous and covered everything I could think of, including a "goodness" score. Here's a copy of the first one I officially recorded:

```
            P R O J E C T    U H O T I

S/N: 0001       KEY WORDS: Earth ground for Mac      Score: 8

WHEN: CA 1955
WHERE: Lemmon Ave plant, Dallas
WHO: Earl McDonald, Jim Nygaard

SUMMARY: Mac complains about lack of a real "earth ground"
when checking out low-level test sets. Nygaard brings him a
cup of dirt with a wire hanging out of it. Weeks later
Nygaard notices cup of dirt with wire hooked to test set
being built. Nygaard laughs at Mac, who, without saying
anything, unhooks cliplead from cup wire and oscilloscope
goes crazy with 60 Hz pickup.



SIMILAR TO/RELATED TO:

TOLD BY: Ed Millis        DATE: 6/18/91
ENTERED: EM 6/18/91

STORY:

 Attachment: Earl (Mac) McDonald keeps bugging Jim Nygaard
the boss about the lack of a good earth ground in the
engineering area where he's designing and building low-level
transistor test sets. Mac says he needs it because he can't
get all the "hum" (60 Hz pickup) out of the sets without one.
Since this would involve a modest sum of money to drill a
hole through the floor and install a real "earth ground,"
Nygaard, as usual, tells Mac to forget it. Mac doesn't forget
and continues to bug Nygaard.

Nygaard one day tells Mac that he's going to get his wish for
an earth ground. He then pulls out a paper coffee cup filled
with dirt with a bare wire sticking out of the dirt. Here's
your earth ground, he says. Let's not hear anymore about your
needing anything.
```

3

Several weeks later Nygaard notices Mac has the coffee cup of dirt sitting on his hutch shelf with a cliplead from the test set that he's working on going to the wire. Nygaard laughs and says "Very funny, Mac." Mac then, without a word, reaches over and takes the cliplead off the "earth ground," with the result that his oscilloscope trace turns to garbage from 60 Hz hum, just as it would if you removed the ground from the system. Mac, of course, has secretly rigged the coffee cup "earth ground" with a real ground wire where it can't be seen, and waited patiently for Nygaard to notice it.

Every week or two I'd take the recorder out of the car and in to the computer and transcribe and expand each of my notes into a page or two in the database. The database file was titled "UHOTI," which is the acronym for "Unauthorized History of Texas Instruments." I was all set, and continued this collection routine regularly for about two years. In the process I eventually "trapped" 129 stories about my life at TI.

What a great collection of data! But for what? I had not the faintest idea of how to turn this database into... into... into *what*? Anything at all? 129 mostly unrelated stories? So they moldered in the hard drive of my computer for years. Every now and then I'd add a story or two, but basically the stories of my life at Texas Instruments that I wanted to save for posterity had, in fact, been saved and were now waiting for me to decide what to do with them. And I hadn't the foggiest.

My retirement from TI in the spring of 1989 led to ten more years of career, only this time as a consultant, or contract engineer, with a couple of companies. It was even more fun than working as an employee of TI. But this time my second and final case of career burnout was caused by driving to and from Allen, Texas, on North Central Expressway. And as I was beginning to develop this ultimate burnout in the spring of 1999, my dear friend Harry Waugh did something that changed my life. He gave me a copy of the book he had written entitled *The Ajax Chronicles*. This neat little book, with the "cookbook" plastic finger binding from Kinko's and Harry's smiling face on the cover, was his story of growing up. I was fascinated by it and read it through to the back cover the first day.

It only took a few milliseconds for me to decide that I had to do what Harry had done so well—write a book of my childhood and youth. The fact that I knew nothing about writing was of no consequence. I could learn. I bought a newer and more modern tape recorder and began the trapping and collection process all over again, only this time it was stories about my childhood and youth. I was committed to writing a book, good or bad, for my friends and relatives, even though they hadn't asked.

I had found earlier that a recollection didn't require a long-winded description in two pages, or three paragraphs, or even one paragraph. A sentence or two could capture the event nicely and sometimes only a couple of key words. This could trigger my brain at any time in the future to total recall. Well, semi-total recall… So I scrapped the over-engineered form that I had used for UHOTI and merely made a list of recollections and key events that occurred in my youth.

Incidentally, during this process I ran across another device that made collecting easier. It was a tiny tapeless voice recorder that was smaller than a deck of playing cards and would fit easily in my shirt pocket. I love electronic gadgets.

A comment about the "incidents and recollections lists" that I've been talking about is probably in order. The giant full-page form I used for the UHOTI memories really had a different long-range purpose than the short one-liners I began using for my childhood memoirs. When I began the UHOTI list, I did not know its ultimate purpose, other than to save the stories of the early days of TI. Maybe someone else would write a book using them, since I seemed to lack the necessary skills. An item on that first list had to be more than a tickler for my brain, it had to be the whole bloody story in as much detail as I could recall. They were put down in an economical, abbreviated style, but were such, I hoped, that someone else could take them and make stories out of them. But now I was going to write a book. *I* was going to, and all I needed to write a story was the memory-jogger of a sentence or even just a couple of words, like "Hugh Jr/clockworks." These words eventually generated a full-page story in my childhood book.

Here's one page of my list transcribed from the tape recorder. They are in the order that I remembered them and put them on tape. They bear no relation to each other, except that talking one memory into the recorder might trigger another event memory. The first item on my list was dated April 12, 1999, probably a couple of days after I finished reading Harry's watershed book.

1. Camp Wisdom, playing "capture the Alamo" in an old stone house when I was a Cub Scout.

2. Craig and Hugh convincing me that my idea for making a light bulb out of a hairpin was a really good one.

3. Summer trip to Philmont Scout Ranch, during the war, in the 1934 Chevrolet school bus.

4. At Philmont, the hike to Old Baldy mountain.

5. At Philmont, the famous coat hanger trick in the three-holer outhouse.

6. Boy Scout stuff in Dallas, like when we tied the dummy on the front bumper of Mr. Richardson's Plymouth.

7. The visits to Graham and playing with my cousins, Spencer Street and Norman Stovall.

8. Building stuff in general, probably a whole chapter – model airplanes, radios, and everything else.

9. The bicycle fitted with the Model T Ford spark coil and battery. My encounter with Waid Dean.

10. When I ran off at the age of 4 or 5 down to McMillan to ride the streetcar downtown.

11. Building the "shocker" out of a bell transformer and No. 6 dry cells, putting it in a Kraft cheese box and taking it to school.

My last entry in this series, Number 133, is dated September 7, 1999, and it was pared to the bone—"Permissive mother and permissive upbringing." That would be good for several paragraphs in Chapter Four, "Pop and Mother." This item was recorded seven days after my last day of work as a consultant. I was now free of the earthly constraints of a job (and also of getting paid) and was off and not only running, but I had achieved take-off velocity as well.

I had generated a swell list of things that happened to me while I was growing up and I was going to write a book from them. But now what? Just like the TI stories, I didn't know what to do with 133 items on a list. How could I turn *that* into a book? And my takeoff was so good...

Chapter 2 – framing it up

If I were writing a book, it would seem that an outline or a framework of some sort would be good. I had collected the details I needed for a book, but it was time to back up, way back, and look at the overall view of this so-called book. And the most obvious outline or framework that books have is the list of chapters. A list of the proposed chapters, in what I would deem to be the appropriate order, would form a framework to build the book on. Perfect. And the good news is that chapters and their order are just words on paper and can be readily changed during the course of writing.

The first step in making such a framework would be to sort out the recollections and incidents into groups of similar things, by time period or type of activity or other criterion. Since I used Microsoft Word to write with, I'll tell you how I "grouped" the stories. You may find some other way as good or better. It makes no difference—you just need a method of moving lines of words.

Since I had cleverly double-spaced my list of 133 Things That Happened To Me, it was simple using Word to highlight an item and either cut-and-paste or drag-and-drop it beneath a similar item. Voila! I now had two related items that would certainly be in the same chapter in my book, next to each other. I continued this through my list, breaking out and identifying groups as they become visible.

If you're not using a computer, or don't like the drag-and-drop deal, just begin sticking an identifying letter by the items, like all the entries relating to "Going to church" are marked *A*, and those about "High School," *B*.

It will become obvious that there are a bunch of natural groupings of the items. One group that popped out early in my list were things related to Boy Scouting. It's a clear chapter choice, even though it extends over a period of several years and would overlap, time-wise, other entries in the book. So I now have *Chapter ? — The Boy Scouts*. That's one.

Since books need several chapters at least, go ahead and continue the process of "bunching" the incidents and descriptions and generating chapters. With any luck, you can soon complete the preliminary outline of the book as far as the list of chapters. And the good news is that they are just marks on paper or in your computer, and if you want to shuffle them around later, or combine two that really weren't big enough to stand alone, you can, and with great ease.

This step of generating the list of chapters for the book may be the single most important. Just like the steel framework of a building basically defines what the building will look like, the framework of chapters defines quite nicely the book you're going to write. Take your time and do it right. You'll know when it's finished. It'll look right and feel right.

As an example, in my childhood book, I clustered the items that I wanted to go into the chapter of my Boy Scout experiences and added annotations. They were not yet in the proper order for writing the chapter, and a partial list of the final 17 items looked like this:

Finding the cache of stuff about scouting – summary of it?

At Philmont, climbing the tree and having a hand-hold break off. What the guy in the outhouse said later.

Camp Wisdom, playing "capture the Alamo" in an old stone house when I was a Cub Scout. Hugh Jr. says "You've killed him."

At Philmont, the famous coat-hanger trick in the three-holer outhouse

Summer trip to Philmont, during the war, in the 1934 Chevrolet school bus. Bad tires and not enough gas ration coupons.

At Philmont, the hike to Old Baldy mountain.

Boy Scout stuff in Dallas, like when we tied the dummy on the front bumper of Mr. Richardson's Plymouth.

Dr. Wallace, Boy Scout physician

The Boy Scout campouts with the Stag Patrol, around White Rock Lake, by bicycle. Also out Greenville Ave. Trains at night.

Jumping off the freight car, getting caught by the railroad police.

Stag Patrol – Bobby Little, Jack and Jim Hanshaw, Jack Godbold, Tom and Hayne Reese, Jerry (?)

Now is the time to get the rest of the material together for your upcoming masterpiece. Every person has his historical treasure trove: old photos, letters, things handed down, and personal memorabilia. Do you have any special things from your youth? Things that you were especially fond of? Or secret things? A model airplane engine, a diary, an A+ book report, a lucky coin, your discharge papers? Gather them up, at least as a description on paper, and see if anything belongs in the narrative of your book. Something that was your favorite will also be the reader's favorite. The reader is interested in what was important to you. Add the items to your list and sort them accordingly.

It's also time to pull together another bit of framework data. Just exactly when did your life occur? When did you start grade school? Or move to Seattle? Or fall down and knock your front tooth out? Or get promoted to sergeant? It was necessary for me to make a time line of my youth. And this process of reliving your past will surely trigger more memories as you painfully flog your brain along from one year of your story to the next. Mine looked like this:

Time	Grade	Age	School/Work/Summer
1935/36	1st	6/7	Robt. E. Lee Elem
1936/37	2nd	7/8	Robt. E. Lee Elem
1937/38	3rd	8/9	Robt. E. Lee Elem
1938/39	4th	9/10	Robt. E. Lee Elem
1939/40	5th	10/11	Stonewall Jackson Elem
1940/41	6th	11/12	Stonewall Jackson Elem
1941/42	8th	12/13	Alex W. Spence Jr. High
1942/43	9th	13/14	Alex W. Spence Jr. High
Summer of 1943		14	Packed Baylor Med School
1943/44	Soph	14/15	North Dallas High School
Summer of 1944		15	Philmont Scout Ranch
1944/45	Junior	15/16	North Dallas High School
Christmas vacation 1944?		15	Stoneleigh-Maple Terrace
Summer of 1945		16	Philmont Scout Ranch
After school 44/45?		15/16	Austin Stanton, GrnvlleAve
1945/46	Senior	16/17	North Dallas High School – Grad
Summer of 1946		17	Varo Mfg, Stanton's garage
1946/47	Fresh	17/18	The Rice Institute
Summer of 1947		18	Vacolite Hearing Aid Co

1947/48	Soph	18/19		The Rice Institute
Summer of 1948			19	Vacolite Hearing Aid Co
1948/49	Junior	19/20		The Rice Institute
Summer of 1949			20	Varo Mfg. Co., new building
1949/50	Senior	20/21		The Rice Institute – Graduated
June 1950			21	National Geophysical
August 1950			21	Geophysical Service Inc.

This was an easy time line to do, and all I needed for my childhood book. The time line for my TI work experience was a different matter. It was incredibly difficult to piece together my history over the 37 years that I was employed. I didn't save a lot of papers from my career, but I found after much digging and sorting that I had saved just barely enough to put a time line together. Well, almost. I could remember well enough building a particular piece of equipment, but about as often as not, I couldn't remember exactly when I did it, and it would take a lot of poring over old organizational charts and memos to home in on it.

In one exasperating time period, I flat ran out of information and could not sort it out. Rather than taking the easy way out and mumbling about it, I called Lee Blanton, fellow TIer, who was casting his magical spell on circuit designs in our engineering section in the era in question. Lee not only remembered exactly when, where, who and why we designed and built everything, he volunteered to draw up the schematics if I needed them. It was an awesome display of mental ability, and Lee solved my problem in short order. And I didn't have to mumble.

I relate this because I don't want you to think that asking someone else to clarify something for your book is cheating. During the writing of my TI book, I took the opportunity of calling a number of old and dear friends, and asking them about something that puzzled me as I was writing. Sometimes they could pull me out of my dilemma and sometimes not, but in any case I had a chance to talk to a friend I hadn't talked to in years. I always won.

One reason I worked so hard on my Texas Instruments time line was that I had the bright idea that it would be neat to put the year on the top of every page of text. The reader could then see at a glance just when the story was happening. Since my book was a pure serial time sequence of events, this seemed like practical idea, so I did it. It was a *lot* of work, both to get the years correct, and to get @#%& Microsoft Word to put it in the right places, but I'm glad I did.

So it's time, if you'll pardon the expression, to get all the chapters identified, sorted out, and in a neat, orderly column, at least for a first pass. Here are a few general ideas for chapter content in a growing-up book, although when you bunch up your incidents, the groups will automatically suggest chapter headings:

- A description of your parents, what they came from, what they did, what they looked like, etc.
- The neighborhood where you grew up, neighbors, stores, schools
- Growing up and interfacing with siblings and/or neighbor kids
- The house you grew up in, moves to other houses, cities
- Travels, vacations, trips
- Going to school and/or college, favorite subjects, hated subjects, teachers, grades, graduation
- Things you joined, like Scouts, Indian Guides, baseball teams, soccer
- Your very earliest memories
- Special interests while growing up
- Your first date, or experiences with the opposite sex

This is going to be your book, not mine, and I've probably overstepped my bounds by even suggesting subjects for chapters. You can do a lot better than I can, since you know what information you want to cover in your book. And your book will be just the way you think it should be, not the way I wrote mine. Don't ever forget—this is *your* book and you can write it any way you want.

What I'm doing is suggesting *one way* to write a book, in a reasonably orderly fashion, that worked for me. But when you get into the actual writing, it's your baby. If you want to write it in all caps using the passive voice, or select an unreadably cute cursive font to print it in, have at it. This is your big chance. But I'm going to make it easier for you to achieve this goal of writing a book, and it will be a book that will flow and please the reader with the organization. If done properly, and I hope that we can both do it properly, the structure of the book will be invisible to the reader. That's the goal to shoot for—the stories and the chapters will flow seamlessly from Chapter One to The End, and the reader will be unable to put your book down. Well, maybe not quite *that* seamless, but you see what I'm driving at.

The structure of the book is important for the reader and even more important for the writer. If the material for a chapter is laid out—the incidents, the descriptions, the dialog—even roughly—then the writing is a piece of cake. You may quote me on this: "It ain't the writing that's hard, it's the deciding what to write about…"

My pre-writing guidelines

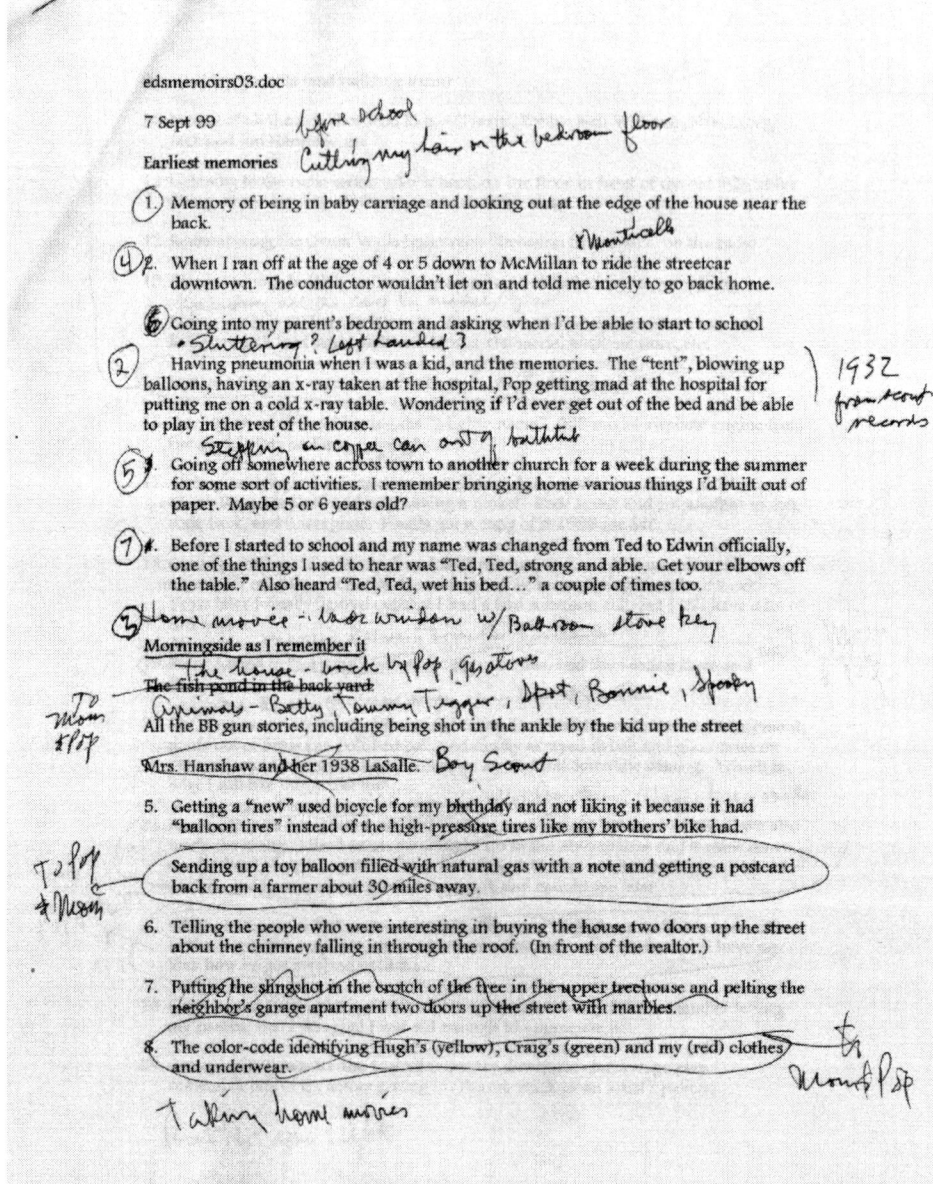

edsmemoirs03.doc

7 Sept 99

Earliest memories *before school Cutting my hair on the bedroom floor*

1. Memory of being in baby carriage and looking out at the edge of the house near the back.
   Montreal?

② 2. When I ran off at the age of 4 or 5 down to McMillan to ride the streetcar downtown. The conductor wouldn't let on and told me nicely to go back home.

⑥ Going into my parent's bedroom and asking when I'd be able to start to school
   • Stuttering? Left handed?

② Having pneumonia when I was a kid, and the memories. The "tent", blowing up balloons, having an x-ray taken at the hospital, Pop getting mad at the hospital for putting me on a cold x-ray table. Wondering if I'd ever get out of the bed and be able to play in the rest of the house.   *) 1932 } from scout records*

   Stepping in copper can out of bathtub
⑤ Going off somewhere across town to another church for a week during the summer for some sort of activities. I remember bringing home various things I'd built out of paper. Maybe 5 or 6 years old?

⑦ Before I started to school and my name was changed from Ted to Edwin officially, one of the things I used to hear was "Ted, Ted, strong and able. Get your elbows off the table." Also heard "Ted, Ted, wet his bed…" a couple of times too.

Home movies - last window w/ Bathroom stove key
Morningside as I remember it
The house - built by Pop, gas stoves
The fish pond in the back yard.
Animals - Betty, Tammy, Tigger, Spot, Bonnie, Spooky
All the BB gun stories, including being shot in the ankle by the kid up the street   *To mom & pop*

Mrs. Hanshaw and her 1938 LaSalle. *Boy Scout*

5. Getting a "new" used bicycle for my birthday and not liking it because it had "balloon tires" instead of the high-pressure tires like my brothers' bike had.

   To Pop & Mom (Sending up a toy balloon filled with natural gas with a note and getting a postcard back from a farmer about 30 miles away.)

6. Telling the people who were interesting in buying the house two doors up the street about the chimney falling in through the roof. (In front of the realtor.)

7. Putting the slingshot in the crotch of the tree in the upper treehouse and pelting the neighbor's garage apartment two doors up the street with marbles.

8. The color-code identifying Hugh's (yellow), Craig's (green) and my (red) clothes and underwear.   *to Mom & Pop*

Taking home movies

After clustering the stories/incidents/vignettes for the chapters, and remembering more in the process, it's time to put them in the order of writing. This would also be a good time to add in notes about descriptions that should be incorporated into the text. An example of my final product, the "pre-writing" guidelines for the first chapters of my childhood book, is on the previous page. The circled numbers show the intended writing order. I had put in few notes about descriptions, but added them as I wrote, kind of *a cappella.*

Looking back at what I finally wrote, I stuck pretty well with this guide, but changed and added things as I wrote. I was learning, too.

Certainly, fleshing out the incidents and interleaving them with descriptions helps the rhythm of the prose. Too much of one or the other makes Jack a dull book. A long string of descriptions reads like a laundry list, and a long string of things that happened reads like, well, like a long list of things that happened. I think readers like a mixture of the two.

I changed my mind about where a couple of the incidents would be in the book—I moved them to other chapters as seemed appropriate. And I scratched a couple of notes entirely. Stay flexible while you're writing, or at least be selectively wishy-washy.

Here's my writing that resulted from the penciled note "Stuttering? Left handed?"

> Somewhere in this pre-school time, my parents decided I should become right-handed. This is what I was told much later, and changing a child's handedness was commonly done at that time. Being right-handed was much preferred to left-handedness. In grade school, for example, the inkwells were on the right side of the desks in a rather obvious display of prejudice. I suspect that I'd been showing signs of left-handedness, but I was going to become right-handed. Otherwise the inkwells would be on the wrong side.
>
> I don't remember the details of the process but I remember that I began to stutter. I stuttered for several years and then outgrew it, or whatever the brain does. This did have a minor lasting effect—I still stutter on a few words that begin with certain letters. My brain wiring had fixed itself except for a few stray nodes. I just avoid those nodes by not using the words. For example, you won't hear me start a sentence with "Iditerod" or not very well, anyway. Fortunately it doesn't come up very often.
>
> So now I'm right handed. Well, mostly. Years later I discovered that my left ear and left eye are dominant which I suspect relates back to my original brain wiring. This is not a

problem except in shooting target rifles, which I did for a while. I really couldn't twist my head around properly and use my left eye on most target rifles. But I tried. For competition shooting I learned to use my right eye. Maybe I can use that as an excuse for my lousy rifle scores. Competition pistol shooting (Metallic Silhouette), however, was better. I could use my left eye easily enough and did pretty well. It still seems natural.

But I seem to have forgotten something. Neither of us knows how to write yet.

Chapter 3 – getting words on paper

Before we begin learning how to write, we should decide what method of writing we're going to use. I'm sure a lot of people have computers, although the generation most likely to write their memoirs is also the most likely not to have them. What to do? Go ahead anyhow, anyway you can. Certainly generating your book in digital form by using a computer is the easiest, but it's not the only way.

Here are some methods of getting your thoughts on paper:

Computer
>Word processing or Publishing program
>>Keyboard input
>>>Touch typist
>>>Non-touch typist
>>Audio input?

Typewriter
>Typed output transcribed to computer word processor by others
>Printed as typed

Pen and paper
>Transcribed to computer word processor
>Printed as written

Audio recording, transcribed to computer or typewriter

Let's begin with the highest-tech and the most commonly used writing method, which is putting your thoughts into a computer via the keyboard. It's also the method that I used and am most familiar with, and so will be what you'll hear most about. But, once again, it is not the *only* way to write a book. You can write a book by any of the above methods, depending on your circumstances and physical constraints. The only thing you really need is that compelling desire to get the story out of your memory and onto paper. You *can* and *will* find a way.

I have written my stories and most everything else in the recent past with an IBM-compatible computer using Microsoft Windows and Microsoft Word. Why? Because Windows came with the computer and I was using Word at the office. I never bothered looking for anything else.

But it has not been a happy relationship. I've now written three books using Word, and have grown used to it. Not fond of it, nor even very comfortable with it, but used to it. It is an almighty powerful program, and in the hands (or should I say fingers?) of a skilled practitioner (which I am not) will do ten times more than I'll ever need. A good Word instruction book, like the one Que publishes, now sitting by my elbow, is about the size of a Philadelphia phone book and needs every page. I have spent equal amounts of time learning how to make Word *do* things, and learning how to make it *quit* doing things. And I still can't make it quit doing some irritating things, but I did finally kill that damn paper clip.

Now that I've aired my petulance about my love-hate relationship with Word, I'll say that it's still my choice for writing, kind of by default. At the time of this writing, it's Word 97, and I will resist upgrading to the last keystroke. Yeah, right…

But Word was not my digital book printer's choice. While I was dealing with him on printing and binding *TI, the Transistor, and Me*, he told me earnestly that if I was going to be a serious writer (whatever that is), I should learn Adobe PageMaker. It could do a lot more things than Word, and his digital printing equipment was *much* happier with it than with Word. He assured me I could easily learn PageMaker in a few months of night study at the local junior college. I then assured *him* that the only practical solution to this problem was for *him* to teach his lousy-ass printing equipment to get along with Word, because the odds of my learning PageMaker were less than zero. More about dealing with book printers in Chapter 11.

Other popular word processors are WordPerfect by Corel Corporation, and the lightweight one that comes with Microsoft Works, commonly supplied with new computers. I have no experience with WordPerfect, but it's highly regarded. The Works word processor is, as I understand it, a stripped-down version of Word, which has some appeal to me.

And if you're a real pro, you have and know how to use PageMaker or FrameMaker or one of the really powerful desktop publishing programs. I understand that they will do absolutely anything, but since I'm barely able to maintain control of Word, it wouldn't do for me to try to step up. The printing companies will love you for it, however, since these programs present a much more robust interface to the printing equipment.

Okay, let's assume at this point you have somehow acquired the use of a computer with a word processor. Are you ready to go? No? You don't know how to type? Let's try a little exercise and see if you can or not. Look down at the keyboard and find the key with the letter *i* on it. [Hint—it's below the *8* and *9* number keys.] Find another key marked "*shift.*" Hold down the shift key with your left index finger and push the *i* with your right. Now press the space bar, which is the long bar beneath the *xcvbnm* line of keys. Find and press, in sequence, the keys marked *c, a,* and *n.* Do the spacebar again. Finish up by pressing the *t, y, p,* and *e,* followed by the period key [lowest row, right side.] Now look at the computer screen. It's a miracle! You can type!

I am one of the fortunate who took touch typing in high school and used it enough to become proficient. The fact that I was the only male in the second semester of the class was just an added bonus. Back then, men didn't type. They didn't need to, because the ladies typed for them. Not so any more. Now, everybody knows how to work a keyboard, at least if they're under 30.
Touch typing is a handy skill but not a requirement for writing a book. My writer and artist daughter Bev took typing in high school, but it didn't take. She now types, quite rapidly and accurately, with four fingers. And no, it's not two on each hand like a normal person, but three fingers on the right and one on the left. I neglected to ask her how she arrived at this asymmetrical method, but for her, it works. She's written something over a million words of prose with this system so who am I to question it?

If, at my age, I were faced with typing up my life story without prior keyboard skills, I probably wouldn't learn to touch type. It's too much trouble to learn, even with the advent of the Mavis Beacon Teaches Typing software by The Learning Company. You might have more spunk and elect to spend the time to learn this useful skill. But for *writing*, which comes out of the brain, staring at the keyboard is not a problem. If you were transcribing a page of longhand, it would be. Secretaries, if such a position actually exists today, need to be able to type without looking at the keyboard. You, as a writer, do not.

Speaking of typing, let me mention a friend of mine, also an ex-TIer, who is writing his memoirs. He has a progressive nerve disease, and can type on his computer keyboard only by clutching a pencil in one hand and typing one letter at a time with the eraser end. He was over 300 pages, about 120,000 words, when I talked to him today. That's how I know *you* can type.

For what it's worth, and I don't know the answer, there are some audio input programs that will translate spoken words into computer text. According to the local computer store, ViaVoice by IBM is the most popular voice-to-text software. Also on the shelf were Dragon's Naturally Speaking and the L&H Voice Express. Prices ranged from $30 to $200. If circumstances warrant, they would be worth a look. My diligent friend who types with a pencil eraser tried one and was not able to get it to work satisfactorily. He thought maybe his East Texas accent screwed it up.

I'll also mention the AlphaSmart, which is a gadget more like a huge pocket calculator than a computer. This device, about the size of a laptop computer, has a full-sized keyboard with a small four-line liquid crystal black and white text display. It's not a substitute for a computer, but it's a minimal and portable text generator that I've found very useful as an accessory. All you can do is type and edit with it, up to about 100 single-spaced pages. Then you can hook a cable from it to your computer and transfer what you wrote into Word or whatever. I bought one to use when I'm traveling and want to write. Very simple, robust, and about one-tenth the cost of a laptop. You can find out about them at www.alphasmart.com/

Going down the pecking order of keyboard-input machinery, the typewriter (for those of you who remember what a "typewriter" is) is the last stop. Not many years ago, the typewriter was the official high-tech instrument for the writer. If the typewriter is your tool of preference now, for whatever reason, full speed ahead on your stories. There are later choices of having your typed pages converted into computer text by a friend or hired gun, or even by a scanner equipped with OCR Optical Character Recognition, software. These systems are getting quite good and, if the typing is in a known font recognizable by the OCR program, it can be converted almost flawlessly into a computer text file. And there is the simplest approach of merely sending the typed originals to the printing company to be directly copied for your books.

But you can't use the excuse that you don't have a computer or a typewriter to avoid writing your book. A yellow pencil and a Big Chief tablet will work, as well as anything else that will put words in a form that someone else can decipher. Another possibility is to tape record your stories while reclining in an easy chair or alongside the pool. You'll need someone to type your audio tapes or Big Chief pages into a computer for you later, but that's not the main thing. And as I learned recently, "The main thing is to keep the main thing the main thing…" *Capturing your story* is the main thing

And just how long is this "story capturing" going to take? I mentioned my friend who has typed 120,000 words with the end of a pencil. Is that inspiring to the novice writer or daunting? *120,000 words? I'll never in a million years type, write or otherwise get that many letters on paper.* Well, let me try to scope out your upcoming task.

Do you know what you want to write about? Have you defined the time period for this epic work? Are you long-winded or short-winded? You can make a great piece of your personal history in a *lot* less than 120,000 words. My entire childhood through college only took 65,000 words.

Suppose you write 1000 words a day, which will print out as two or three single-spaced pages. In a month you'll have 30,000 words and a nice piece of work. In fact, for certain types of personal stories, that just might be all the way to *The End*. You've written 75 pages. See? It didn't take all that long. *Write as much as* you *want to write.*

I'm a pretty fast writer, and it took me three months to write the 105,000 words of the first draft of my TI book, including doing all my lists, sorting out stories, looking up names and the other peripheral work. But then, it required another three months to unscramble my sentences and commas in the editing mode. Such is the problem of fast writers. Half-fast would be a better description of my style.

Chapter 4 – how to write without knowin nuthin

Learning to write is like learning to swim by jumping off a pier into deep water. I don't think it works very well for swimming, but it's the only way to learn to write. Just jump in.

I finally had all my recollections in neat order, grouped into chapters and interspersed nicely with descriptions. It was time to write. Gulp. I was afraid of that. So late one night, after stalling as long as I could, I took a deep breath, cracked my knuckles, and sat down at the keyboard. I was ready to try writing something. I picked a single vivid incident from my youth: "Craig and Hugh Jr. convincing me that my idea for making an electric light bulb out of a hairpin was a really good one…" And believe me, it was a vivid memory. I wrote something like this:

> "The sharing of 'really good ideas' by Craig and Hugh Jr. with me began early. They began before I had achieved the proper defensive posture that came later, with experience. Bad experience, generally! This notable incident began innocently enough on the carpeted floor of Pop and Mother's bedroom, where we were playing some childish game. But also on the floor were a few spare parts from Mother's Singer sewing machine. I became intensely interested in a part of this sewing machine— the removable lamp.
>
> This particular shiny, chrome-plated electrical device was of interest to me because it lacked a lamp bulb, but was otherwise intact and functional. It occurred to me that if I could make a light bulb for it, I'd have a very useful object. In some strange way I think I knew how light bulbs worked, with the electricity passing through a loop of wire inside the glass globe and lighting it up because it got really hot. *Really* hot! Since I wasn't in the first grade yet, I might have gotten this great idea from one or both of my helpful brothers.

…and it goes on and on for several more long paragraphs.

Let me diverge for a minute and bring up something I found interesting, and I think you'll find it not only interesting but encouraging. As I began struggling to write, and sorting out what had happened, and how, and where, memories I thought I had forgotten came back to me. I began writing this first little story with a minimal, if traumatic, recollection of what happened to me on the floor of the bedroom so many years before. But as I began grasping at the ideas to put on paper, other memories began coming back—the vision of the gas stove next to me, the peculiar braided cover of the electric cord on the light socket, the slick feel of the shiny chrome reflector, and of course, the expectant looks on the faces of my cruel brothers as they ran out of the room. It was truly amazing, and it happened time after time as I wrote, and I'm sure it will happen to you, also.

Several times people have told me how wonderful my memory must be, and how they couldn't remember half what I did. Baloney. When you sit down to write, not forgetting to crack your knuckles first, there will be more coming out of your brain than you ever believed was in there. Trust me.

Finishing the first little piece of trial writing gave me a nice sense of accomplishment. When I later completed my first whole chapter, I had a really great sense of accomplishment, and when I finally finished the book, *the whole book*, and typed "The End," I can't describe the feeling. All you have to do is write your book and you can have that feeling, too. Your reward is waiting. Trust me again.

The elation of completing my first trial story for the book was dampened somewhat by my two critics, er, editors—dear friend Shirley Sloat (AKA "The Dreaded Red Pencil") and my dear daughter Bev Haskin, experienced writer and artist. The efficiency of email allowed me to whiz this minor literary marvel off to them minutes after I'd finished it. The efficiency of email also brought back two noticeably lukewarm reviews. Bev's was especially descriptive, with something about sticking her finger down her throat. But I was truly blessed by having two smart people with different backgrounds and ages take the time to read my first writing experiment and comment honestly on it. I didn't know how to write and I needed their guidance, and I still do.

You, too, need to find someone or two to guide your beginning writing style. If you've written before, this may not be necessary. But for engineers, like myself, who have written little except in bullet outline form for projecting on a screen in a meeting, it's invaluable. Amateur writers, such as you and I, need perspective on what we're writing, and an "outsider" is the best supplier of perspective. Also, it will be useful later if you can enlist their aid in editing your writings. After you get your "writing style" on track, your someone or two can be called on to spot those pesky typos that are all but invisible to the perpetrator. Treat your outsiders nicely. You need their help.

I was searching for a "style" to write my book in, and to make a long story shorter, I rewrote the hairpin piece a number of times. Each time I rewrote it, I took out words and simplified it and made it less cute. Finally, I stopped trying to find a style, and just wrote, and wonderfully enough, the lack of style was just the style I was comfortable with. I sent a piece off to another dear friend, a professional magazine editor and published author, and when she told me it "sounds like you talking," I quit searching and began writing in earnest. Boy, am I glad I didn't have to write in a style.

I might have saved time if I had read Stephen King's *On Writing* before I started. I read it later, and it is a book that I highly recommend. The book is half autobiography, which is fascinating, and half how-to book for writers. To say that he can succinctly tell you how to make your writing better is an understatement. Do *what* with the adverbs, Stephen? It's both entertaining and useful.

I accidentally did most of what Stephen King recommends, like getting rid of most of the adjectives and adverbs, throwing out cute stuff, ixnaying exclamation points except in emergencies, and simplifying the sentences. The little hairpin story read a lot smoother when I was finished. Here's part of the same story, final version:

> "The brotherly interaction was always educational for me. Hugh and Craig were always creative, and Hugh especially read a lot and shared it with us. This sharing of "good ideas" by Craig and Hugh Jr. with me began quite early. We three were playing on the floor of Pop and Mother's bedroom with some parts of Mother's sewing machine (she really was permissive) and I became interested in the removable lamp. This little chrome-plated Singer attachment bolted on the sewing machine and plugged into the wall to make light near the needle. This one was missing the light bulb, and the question came up as to how light bulbs made light...

It has fewer adjectives and adverbs, and the Cuteness Factor is near zero.

While we're talking about writing style, let me give you another illustration. Picture a son taken to the Greyhound bus station by his parents during the early part of WWII. He's joined the army and is leaving for duty. He might write up the experience in his autobiography like this:

> "Three years earlier, I had received my orders to report to boot camp, and my parents took me down to the Greyhound bus station to see me off."

But a classmate of mine from Rice and fellow electrical engineer, lived the experience and wrote it like this:

> "Three years earlier, my mother and father had to stand beside the right rear wheel of a Greyhound bus and watch helplessly as their only son went off to an unknown fate in a bitter world at war."

Now *that* is good stuff. Why do I think it's so good? Because it brings an emotional content into the narrative that was missing in the first writing. Believe me, at the time that bus was driving off, there were a lot of strong emotions whirling around. It really describes the whole moment, way beyond a mere description of the activity. It's just plain good. Maybe Jeff should be writing this book instead of me. He blended another dimension into the description—the feelings of the people who were involved, and it adds immensely to the narrative.

Speaking of adding feeling to writing, treat your work like a chef treats a pot of stew on the kitchen stove. It's up to the chef to stir in the spices and seasonings that take it from the realm of boiled meat and potatoes into a culinary masterpiece, the sight and aroma of which will make your mouth water. It doesn't take a lot of seasonings for a pot of stew, and it doesn't take a lot in the way of words to season your literary work. Every now and then get creative, get crazy, get carried away. Surprise and maybe even shock the reader a little. Just a little.

Chapter 5 – putting one and one together

Let's assume that you've decided to put a dozen incidents and some nice descriptive material in your Chapter Three, entitled "When Sisters Made Me Cry." Now what? How do you tie them together into a cohesive chapter? My first writing, my childhood book, *High Voltage, Gunpowder, and Mousetraps*, wasn't as difficult to "put together" as my Texas Instruments book. My childhood had more continuity than my career at TI.

But I puzzled over this problem of how to string a bunch of incidents together into a readable form, and discussed it several times with daughter Bev. She, a voracious and omnivorous reader, suggested I get a couple of H. Allen Smith books to study. She remembered that *To Hell in a Handbasket, Low Man on a Totem Pole, Lost in the Horse Latitudes*, and *Life in a Putty Knife Factory* were basically dozens of stories of his early days as a newspaper reporter put end to end and made into a book.

I did as she suggested, and I'll suggest the same to you if you have a problem with connectivity. H. Allen Smith does a good job with unrelated stories, but, as you and I will also do, he sometimes just finishes a story and then starts a new and unrelated one in the next paragraph. Nothing wrong with that if there's no better way.

This list of stuff you're going to write about has been saucered and blowed and is ready to go. Except, when you start writing them up, you'll find that some incidents that seemed so good in your mind, stink when put on paper. Or even worse, they sound mean-spirited in print. And some "jokes" don't translate well. Don't hesitate to throw them out and forget about them. I don't think you want mean stuff in your book. Or maybe you do, but I didn't want mean stuff in my book so I purposely left out a few things that were on my list. I suppose a "genuine" autobiography should treat all incidents in the life of the writer with equal emphasis, but not mine. I like the happy and funny stuff, which, blessedly, was the great majority of both my childhood and my career. Your choice. But if unpleasant things or circumstances are important in telling your story, you may feel that you owe it to the reader to put them in.

Kind of along the same line, what should a writer do with "naughty" stories? I think slightly naughty stories, whatever that means, are fine, especially if they're funny. They add a little of that "spice" to the writing, Just spicy enough to put a little flavoring in your book. I don't think most readers would be offended by some naughty recollections, since they probably have a few of their own.

I suggest you study your list of items to be put in a chapter, both the incidents and the descriptive sections, and see if there are any common threads that would make segueing from one into another natural. If the order of "stuff" is not totally nailed down by a time line, rearranging the order of stories and descriptions can sometimes make the transitions easier and more natural.

To illustrate these ideas, here are parts of two stories tied together with only a paragraph break:

> ...and came to see if I was hurt. "Are you okay?" I opened my mouth and made pantomime speech but no sound. Per the standard first-aid ritual of the day, I was laid back down on the ground and my legs pumped against my chest. This soon brought me back to a reasonably normal condition and other than eating off the mantel for a few days, there were no lasting injuries. To my knowledge, no one ever successfully crossed from tree to tree without touching the ground. But Lord knows I tried.
>
> One day I found myself with a problem at the top of our block on Morningside. I had bicycled up the hill and then the chain had jumped off the rear sprocket on the old high-pressure-tired bike. No big deal if you had a wrench, which I didn't, to loosen the rear axle...

I don't think that connection reads well at all. The transition doesn't flow. It just kind of sits there in your path and makes you step over it. Sometimes this is the only way, but for this example, let's try again. The added connecting text is in italics:

> ...and came to see if I was hurt. "Are you okay?" I opened my mouth and made pantomime speech but no sound. Per the standard first-aid ritual of the day, I was laid back down on the ground and my legs pumped against my chest. This soon brought me back to a reasonably normal condition and other than eating off the mantel for a few days, there were no lasting injuries. To my knowledge, no one ever successfully crossed from tree to tree without touching the ground. But Lord knows I tried.
>
> *Lack of stress analysis knowledge was one thing, but it was just plain old lack of good judgment* one day when I found myself with a problem at the top of our block on Morningside. I had bicycled up the hill and then the chain had jumped off the rear sprocket on the old high-pressure-tired bike. No big deal if you had a wrench, which I didn't, to loosen the rear axle...

I think it's a lot better and I like it. And that, my friend, is what really counts in writing my book. *I* like it. It reads smoother and the rock in the road that we had to step over is gone.

Of course, there are a few more things you might want to add to your chapter, like pictures. If you have pictures, by all means put them in your book. The digital printing technology is such that you pay little penalty for pictures. Not like in the bad old times when halftone screens had to be made, at additional cost, for every picture in the book. Now you can scan it and insert it. Piece of cake? Not for me it wasn't. Not with good old MS Word. My *High Voltage, Gunpowder and Mousetraps* has lots of pictures in it, which I like a lot. And every picture was an experience. I was never sure just exactly where the picture was going when I pushed the Insert button. And I don't want you calling me up and trying to explain what I was doing wrong. I *know* I don't understand putting pictures in with the text but I don't want to hear about it now. Sometimes the photos would vanish and show up three or four pages away. It was always exciting to add pictures.

But the end result, regardless of the screwed-up methods I used, was good. Pictures are good. Or, you can weenie out and put all the pictures together on a few pages in the center or end of the book. I personally wanted to have them in with the text, so the reader can see what I was talking about. But it wasn't easy.

For what it's worth, the old "picture is a thousand words" is true. If a description of something gets long and convoluted, maybe you should draw a sketch to explain it. My youth involved "rubber guns," which have been unknown in polite society since about the end of WWII and the beginning of tubeless tires. Rubber guns were featured in several of my favorite childhood stories, so I sat down one evening and sketched up a couple of rubber guns. These were scanned into pictures for the book. Things that are lost and gone forever should be documented, even if it's just a homemade, freehand sketch. Or maybe *especially* if it's a homemade, freehand sketch. A sketch by you, the author, adds yet another dimension to your work.

I did the same type of "visual aid" for the description of my neighborhood—my growing-up stomping grounds. My brain still held the "map" that was burned into it as a child, and I transferred it to a piece of paper. It was a familiar and wonderful map, even if the top was east and north to the left. That's the way it was in my brain, and I certainly wasn't going to change it now. The map, with added notations where some of the important events of my young life occurred, was put in with the "front matter" of the book as a reference.

While I'm on the subject, I also put a simple genealogy chart as another reference in the front matter. It showed the relationships of some the people I talked about in the book. *Now let's see—Aunt Agnes was my mother's sister? Right?* Of *course* she was!

I've run out of things to help get your memoirs on paper. Here's a summary of the ideas:

- Gather your stories and other material with some type of "trapping mechanism" *religiously,* and I don't mean only on Sundays

- Do a time line of the period of your life you're writing about

- Sort the one-liners into groups that may become chapters

- Decide on tentative chapter headings and the one-liners to go in each

- For each chapter, sort the one-liners into the order you want to write about them

- Add descriptions as desired

- Practice writing one or two stories to gain confidence

- Practice hooking stories together

- Write the book, one chapter at a time

- Edit the tar out of it, preferably with help

When you've done that, you've done the hard part. You've got your story on paper. You're over the hump and definitely airborne and climbing out. You, my friend, are an author.

Some more unsolicited advice: put your text aside and go on with the next steps of putting your book together. Don't even think about what you've written. Just let it alone and quit picking at it. Get totally involved in the finishing processes and have fun doing them. Then, and only then, go back through your manuscript with a fine-toothed eye.

I believe Stephen King recommends a six-week moratorium on looking at what you've written before you do the *final* final run-through. If you truly edited the tar out of your book, you're just about burned out with it. It's starting to look stale and doubts about your writing abilities are waking you up in the middle of the night. At least, that's your perception and it's wrong. Wait as long as you can and then do a final edit. Few of us can wait six weeks before running off to the printers with our newborn, but any amount of wait time is better than today. You will be pleasantly surprised with your final edit. *By golly, that's a pretty good story!*

Next comes the mechanical part of making your book look like a real book, and read like a real book. It's time to edit, and to do something about the spelling, grammar, punctuation, and "style." You'll want to add some additional sections, and do a lot of other fussy things. But the good news is, you've written your book, and the information you've wanted to save is down on paper. This tidying up is just a bunch of rules that someone else thought up, and your masterwork could live without it, but it puts the icing on the cake.

Following these general rules for writing a book will make you look like a pro, even if you don't think you are. I guarantee you can make your book read slick as a whistle, and look so professional that even the jaded printer who's done dozens of self-published books will take a look at it and say, "Wow, that really looks great!" All you have to do is spend probably as much time as you spent writing it on the process of editing and finishing up your book. Doesn't that have a nice ring to it? *Your book!*

Chapter 6 – the writer's toolbox

Okay, junior writer, you've got a trade to learn. And you need to get some tools to begin your new work. All workmen have tools and you're no exception. You're going to need some books, reference books to be exact, to help you with some things, like:

- Spelling
- Synonyms
- Grammar
- Style

Spelling isn't too hard to figure out. Get a dictionary, new or used, or trust Word's "Spell Checker" if you're using it. Even better, do both if you can. Spell Checker is speedy and although it sometimes doesn't understand the context, it does a good job on the vast majority of words. One minor flaw I've found in Word's Spell Checker is that it occasionally can't decide if two words should be one word, two words or hyphenated. Like, is it "sliderule" or "slide rule," or "slide-rule?" Since you probably won't use those particular words as often as I did in my book, you probably don't care.

But this sort of quandary will come up in your writings, and there's a solution if you want to cut your writing that finely—*One Word, Two Words, Hyphenated?* is an inexpensive, neat book by Mary Louise Gilman, published by the National Court Reporters Association. The title tells it all—it's a list of thousands of words and phrases with the accepted use of spaces and hyphens. Their website at the time of this writing is www.verbatimreporters.com.

This discussion is moot if you're not that picky about the smallest details of spelling. Word's Spell Checker and a nice dictionary will do a perfectly adequate job and nobody (but me) will know if the hyphen belongs or not. By the way, it's "slide rule."

Synonyms. Having a book of synonyms is a lifesaver (life saver? life-saver?) when writing. Especially late at night when you've already used the word "ecstatic" twice in a paragraph and feel a strong urge to use it one more time. What I learned to do was whip open my *The Synonym Finder* by J. I. Rodale to "ecstatic," and pick out another word—"exhilarated," or "orgiastic," or maybe even "happy as a clam at high tide," depending on the level of feeling in the sentence. My edition of Rodale's lists a total of 35 words and phrases to use when I've burned out "ecstatic." A very useful book, indeed, and I think indispensable to a writer. If you already have a version of the evergreen *Roget's*

Thesaurus of Words and Phrases, it'll work, too. I found Rodale's a little easier to use. Words are what this is all about, so have plenty of them available.

Grammar is a sticky wicket for me. I remember little of what I was taught so long ago, but I think I speak a reasonably good brand of English. And that's kind of what I do—I try to write as much like I speak as I can and not get fancy. I also trust Shirley 'Dreaded Red Pencil' Sloat to keep me from straying too far from accepted usage, and lapsing into the present tense when the sentence began in the past tense.

But I think every writer, and this means you, should spend a couple of bucks and a couple of hours and read a thin book, *The Elements of Style* by Strunk and White. This lightweight paperback (light-weight paper-back?)[1] has more good stuff in it per page than any book alive. Written by Oliver Strunk in 1935 and first revised and updated by E. B. White in 1959, it is a true classic. The best summary of it is from a *New Yorker* writer: "The work remains a nonpareil: direct, correct, and delightful." How, you ask, could a book about *grammar* be "delightful?" Read it and become a believer.

Speaking of delightful, there's one other book that describes the general grammar and word usage in writing in a manner that will not only surprise and delight you, but will entertain and teach you. And this marvelous book is *On Writing* by none other than the horror writer, Stephen King. I have already mentioned it in Chapter 4, the section on how to write. Whether you like his horror stories or not, Stephen King is a masterful writer. I didn't know that words on paper could scare the bejeebers out of me, a scare-proof adult, until I read *The Shining* late one night. Let's just say he has a way with words that few people have. He has good, simple and solid advice for writers, with his autobiography thrown in for good measure. Most entertaining and instructive. I learned a lot from it, especially from his advice about coming back through your writings and getting rid of adjectives and adverbs, simplifying your sentences, and "killing your little darlings."

One eye-opener[2] I learned from Mr. King—it's perfectly okay to use just plain "said" when people are talking in your writing. You don't really have to use "expounded" or "remarked" or "opined." Just "said" works. It's an invisible word and nobody will notice if you use it more than once in a paragraph. I felt a *lot* better after reading that. And it's so simple…

---

[1] Okay. I'll quit.

[2] Interestingly enough, *One Word, Two Words…* says that it should be 'eyeopener' and Word's Spell Checker says 'eye-opener' is correct. What's a fellow to do? I think it looks better with the hyphen.

Style. What in Sam Hill is *style*? Well, style is all the little stuff that makes you crazy when you write a book, like:

- Which side of the comma do I put the 'close quote' mark on?
- Should I use all capitals or italics to emphasize a word?
- Should I put one space or two after a period? *(ONE!)*
- Is it elm or Elm, asap or ASAP, rpm or RPM?
- Should I indent or add a blank line and then indent?

If you're like me, you've looked at eight gazillion examples of these in print and can't remember a one. Hence, the style manual. Style manuals have rules for all the little nit-picky things that might (or might not) upset you when you're trying to tune up your book.

Once more I'll say that if it doesn't bother you, the world won't end if you ignore the finer points of book crafting. Remember the main thing—you've got your story on paper. It'll run without a final tune-up, but it'll run better with one.

So if you're of such a mind, run down to your local used bookstore and find a style manual. I have two in front of me. One of them is *A Manual of Style*, by the University of Chicago Press. This book is better known as the "Chicago Style Manual." The other book, my personal favorite, is *A Manual of Style*, prepared by the U.S. Government Printing Office. There's not much difference in the two books, especially in their titles, and there's a flock of others you may find at the bookstore. They are crammed full of interesting and useful things you never thought of.

Another book that deserves mention is *Producing a Quality Family History* by Patricia Law Hatcher, a professional genealogist. This paperback is pointed especially to the serious family historian, and is published by Ancestry Incorporated, Salt Lake City, Utah. All aspects of family history writing and publishing are covered, and when you've outgrown my thin how-to manual, Pat Hatcher's book will carry you light years farther into the details of the world of writing.

As an engineer, I'm used to getting lots of tools for any new job I'm faced with, so my bookshelves are now loaded with swell books about writing. A fellow can't have too many tools *or* books.

There's another handy place to find answers to style questions—go get a book that somebody published and look in it. Amazing! Somebody has already done all this before! I discovered this rather simple solution late one night when I was trying to write my first dialogue. The fact that I'd read other people's writings that were full of dialogue didn't help a bit. When do you indent? What do you do when you change speakers? Can one speaker say two things without separately indenting? It was suddenly like I was inventing writing dialogue. And if the *Manual of Style* had it in there, I couldn't find it. Bright idea. I got a murder mystery and sat down and studied the dialogue. Nothing to it after I looked at it with a writer's eye instead of a reader's eye.

Tuck this away for future use—any book, *any* book, can teach you a lot about style and everything else about putting a book together. And you don't have to tell anybody where you got your great idea for those fancy chapter headings.

The Title was not listed at the beginning of this chapter because I didn't want you to think there were books that could help you generate one. If only there were. It's an important step in the birth of a book, and I have spent more time agonizing over the names of my soon-to-be creations than I have writing some of the chapters. For some reason, titles for the few pieces of fiction I've written just seemed to pop out. Not so for my two books of memoirs, and not so for this little book. At the time of writing, I still don't have a title that I like. I've got about 50 candidates my kids and I have thought up but nothing has really zinged me. So good luck on thinking up a great title for your writings. I have no advice. If you will turn to the front cover of this book, you will see the final outcome of my present quandary. I hope you like it. I hope *I* like it.

Chapter 7 – what goes where?

You just thought you were through writing. Crack your knuckles one more time and pull up a fresh tablet. A book is put together in a formal, standardized fashion, and it would enhance your book if you followed these semi-sacred rules. Yes, you *could* put your title page in the back and the index in the front, but nobody would like it but you. Readers are used to things being in certain places and now's not the time to get creative. You've come this far and obeyed the rules, and it's just a little farther. Control yourself. Later, you can write some science fiction and go berserk, but now you've got to write a few more parts to properly finish your book.

Here is a simplified standard assembly sequence of a book, from front to back. Pick up a book and look at what others have done, and to clarify my brief descriptions.

- **Front cover**. Can be either paper or a "board" for hardback. We'll touch on the design of the cover later.

- **Blank leaf** if hardback only. Or if you do as I did with my lack of knowledge on my first book and supplied the bindery with a blank page before the title, you can start your book off with *two* blank sheets. It looks kind of dumb, actually.

- **Frontispiece.** If you have a frontispiece, like a great family photo, it goes ahead of the title page, and is printed so as to face the title page.

- **Title page**. The front, or odd-numbered side, of the title page has the book title and author's name on it. That's you! It might also include a subtitle if you're so inclined. My second book, *TI, the Transistor, and Me* has the subtitle, *or My Dis-Integrated Circuit Through Texas Instruments*. Quite possibly too cute. The back, the even-numbered side of the title page, carries the copyright (if any), ISBN (discussed later) and printing information.

- **Dedication**. Generally short and sweet, it's on the right side with the back left blank.

- **Foreword**. This is for some other person, who might be an authority, to write an introduction. It could be several pages. But unless you can con one of your parents or a sibling into writing something, this probably won't be used. The writer's name and title should appear at the end, generally in italics.

- **Preface.** You get to tell why you wrote the book. It can lap over to the back and to additional pages if you're long-winded.

- **Acknowledgments.** Feelings of gratitude should be listed along with the names of the gratifiers. Again, use the back and additional pages if your gratitude is boundless.

- **Contents.** Here's the table of contents for your book. It can be just a listing of the chapters and their titles with page numbers, or it might include a brief description that expands on the information in the chapter title. Use the back and more pages if necessary. Actually, I don't suppose you have to give the chapters titles if you don't want to. Just plain old:

Chapter Nine————————————157

tells the reader where to find it, but a chapter title is a bit more useful, like:

9   Our Trip to Europe with Suse...............157

Or even a deluxe version:

Chapter Four—1956-1960...............................54
Onward to Houston!
More transistors? But I said...
We give birth to a CAT, with Nygaard's help

- **Illustrations.** If your book has a lot of illustrations, you could list them and their page numbers. Not many books bother with this.

- **Quotations.** To be *really* fancy, use a right-hand blank page for some exotic quotation from a person nobody ever heard of, preferably in a foreign language. *Bartlett's Obscure Quotations* is a good place to start.

- **Special Stuff.** Here's the location for your special stuff, if you have any. A neighborhood map and an abbreviated genealogy chart went here in my childhood book

- **Introduction.** This is a place for someone, frequently not the author, to lay a little foundation for the upcoming text. I don't think it's needed in a memoirs-type of book, but if you can get Aunt Salmonella to do a summary of the family tree and why you turned out the way you did, it might be entertaining.

And that collection of pages, my friend, is what is known in the book business as the Front Matter. It is generally page-numbered in lower case Roman numbers, like i, ii, iii, iv, etc. which Word can do for you automatically. With the exception of the frontispiece, all of the items above begin on the right-side page of the book, which by definition is an odd-numbered page. If you have a frontispiece, the front side of that page is blank and is considered "i," but the page number is not printed. The frontispiece itself would be marked "ii." It faces the title page. The title page, in this case, would be "iii" but the page number is not generally printed on it. Everybody else gets a Roman numeral as its page number.

All right-hand pages are odd; all left-hand pages are even. After the last bit of Front Matter, Chapter One will start on the next right-hand page which should be numbered "1" in Arabic numbers. And of course, the first book you pick up to see if what I just told you was correct, will have something done differently. There are no concrete rules except in bridge building. When in doubt, do what makes sense and what you think looks best. The Style Patrol won't come knocking on your door in the night and carry you off to the Bad Front Matter dungeon.

The main body of text, namely your book, is added after the front matter with the first page of the first chapter on page 1, which is on the right side of the book. Duh. After that, chapters may begin on either odd or even pages, like either the right or left side of the book. I incorrectly came to the conclusion when putting together my first book that it would really look great if I always started chapters on the right-hand page. And of course, with normal statistics, about half the chapter beginnings have a blank page on their left. It looks really lousy and I can't recall why I thought it would be a good idea. It wasn't.

I casually slipped in the word "copyright" when I mentioned the back of the title page. I think you should fill out the Short Form TX (non-dramatic literary work) and send it to the Library of Congress Copyright Office along with a copy of your book and $30 (at this time). I have two Certificates of Registration, and will soon have a third for this book. Their website is www.loc.gov/copyright, and you can download the form. Just do it, and be sure and take credit for it on the back of the title page.

Of course, there's more stuff to be added after the text. In fact it will take more time than the front matter. Let's get the easy items out of the way first, and then we'll get to the biggie. After the main body of text you may add an **epilogue**, **appendix**, **notes**, **bibliography** and/or **glossary**. But I doubt it. If you have a need for these items, add them in that order and continue the Arabic numbering from the main text. And now for the biggie—the index.

- **The index**

It is my *very strong* feeling that you should put an index in your book. A personal book without an index is like a Slim Jim without a beer. It just ain't natural. The first thing people will do when they pick up your new masterpiece is to thumb through the first few pages, and the second thing is flip back to the index and see if their name or some other person's name is in it. Especially people with genealogical leanings. They're always looking for information about people and places. Do an index. It can be big and complete, with every person, place and incident listed, or it can be a stripped down, people/places only job.

For all my whining about Microsoft Word, it has a great index-maker. The problem I had was learning to use it properly. The built-in help is pretty good, but for me it couldn't replace a book that I could read in a leisurely fashion in my easy chair. So I shopped around for "How to Use Word 97" books and was surprised to find that some of them didn't even mention the indexing function. I settled on the Que, *Using Microsoft Word 97,* and have been very pleased with it.

I first copied my book text "dot doc" file into another file that I could use for practice, since I suspected I would screw up my clean text file learning how to index. Then I read Que and practiced doing what it said, and Voila! I soon had a little index. It works really, really, well. You can make a terrific professional-looking index using the index function in Word. It takes a while to do it right, but worth every minute. And it makes your work look finished and complete.

One word of caution here. Later, you will be messing with the type fonts and sizes and margins and all sorts of things that could affect the number of pages in your book. For example, changing from one font to another, even if it's the same point size, can change the length of your book by pages. And this will screw up your index if you don't recompile it after you've finished all the diddling around with the format. It's a simple keystroke or two, but don't forget to do it as your last act before visiting the printing companies. Another option is to wait until you've completely formatted and paginated your book before you do the index.

Did I hear someone say they're not using Word and a Gigahertz computer, but a hand-me-down Underwood typewriter? I'm glad you called, because you're not going to get off the index hook. Not by a long shot. You don't need no stinking computer to make an index. You use... (pause for effect)...INDEX CARDS!... (Gasp!)   And I can speak from experience that it can be done.

A long, long time ago in 1977, my dear late wife Mary Ruth finished a large book (475 pages) on the history of my mother's family, entitled A *Graham Chronicle*. And she did it with a used IBM Executive typewriter, scissors and glue. Not an IBM Selectric, mind you, but the old hundred-pound job. It, along with a blizzard of papers, occupied our dining room table for two years, and with it she wrote an absolutely marvelous book. After she finally finished it, she was considerably burned out, and when I asked her about the index, her reply was not nice. *Well*, says I, *I'll do the index for you. Since you wrote an entire book about my mother's family, the least I could do would be to index it for you.* So I did. And it took a lot of index cards, but it really wasn't as bad as I thought. Of course, I thought it was going to be *really* bad. You've probably already figured out how to do it, but I'm going to finish my story anyhow.

It's a simple operation, and it gives you a clue as to where the term "index card" came from. Wonder no more. With the main text all finished and the pages numbered in final form, pick the first item on page one that should be in the index.

"...*at the door was our neighbor, Fred Hinkley. We invited him...*"

Write on an index card exactly how you want the index entry to read, and put the page number, "*1*," in the right corner.

"*Hinkley, Fred   1*"   or   "*Hinkley, Frederick C. (neighbor)   1*"

Put that card in an empty card file box. Pick the next item in the text to be indexed and do the same thing, except this time, you must put the card in the file box in alphabetical order. Not too hard—it's either in front of or behind the first card. It gets harder as you go, but you get the idea. After X weeks or months of scrawling on index cards and stuffing them in the file box alphabetically, you finish the last entry on the last page. All you do now is transcribe those million or so index cards in alphabetical order, preferably but not necessarily in two columns, and you have your index.

Chapter 8 – making it pretty

You've done it. You've finished all the writing for your book. Really. Just a few last tidbits and you're ready for the printer's magic. Oh happy day! But now the tidbits—like what is your book going to *look* like when it's printed? The best way I found to answer that question was to make a "sample" book of a few pages and *look* at it. What a revolutionary idea! And the things you'll probably want to fuss with are:

- The **page size** of the finished book.

- The **margins** on the pages, both sides and top and bottom.

- The **main text font**, or type style, and the size of it in "points."

- The **heading fonts**, such as "Chapter One," and "Preface" and stuff like that.

- **Page numbers**, like where on the page?

- **Headers** on each page, like the book title or chapter name?

- **Fancy stuff**, for example, *dropped caps* on the first letter of each chapter.

Page size—One of the major decisions you're going to make is the size of your book. This decision can be affected by a lot of things, such as how many copies you're going to print, and who's going to do it. If, for example, you've decided to print and bind it yourself (after being inspired by a later chapter of this book) it will be a lot easier if your book is 8½ by 11 inches. Why, you ask? Because trimming pages to size is a huge pain in the butt for the home handicrafter. I have the world's best office-type paper trimmer and it will only cut five or six pages at a time without skewing the cut line. I've made up a lot of small books, up to 100 pages (which is 50 sheets of paper, more or less), and it can be done with patience and care. But if you plan to print 20 copies of a 200-page book, forget it. Either do it in the 8½ by 11 format and use the full page, or let the printer or bindery trim and bind it for you after you've done the printing. The next chapter discusses some of these options.

A commonly used page size is 6 by 9 inches. I like it fine and chose it for my first two books. This book is larger, being 7 by 10 inches, mostly because of the illustrations and it just seemed that an "instructional" book should be bigger.

Nice size, isn't it? I exercised my printing company when I was fiddling with my TI book, and got a price from them for making the pages 5 ½ by 8 ½ inches, which you might have deduced as being half of an 8 ½ by 11 sheet. And yes, some of the clever digital printing equipment can split your pages up and print two on a sheet in the proper manner, thus saving some paper. I spent a lot of time reformatting my pages and getting it to fit just right, and then decided I didn't like it. It doesn't sound like it's much smaller than 6 by 9, but to me it seemed a bit too small. It felt more like a commercial paperback size, although it's really bigger.

The price difference didn't give me much incentive, either. It's your call. Whatever blows up your skirt, as they say. The printer/bindery will have to trim your book to *some* size, and trimming it to 7⅛ by 9⅞ inches doesn't cost a dime more than 6 by 9. That's why I'm going to suggest that you mock-up a few pages of your book in several sizes and see how they look and feel to you.

Margins—I was surprised when I flipped through some of the self-published books on display at my printer's office. Did it occur to anyone that the widths of the margins make a huge difference in how a book looks? I mean it makes a *lot* of difference—probably the single biggest factor in what the eye perceives when scanning a book. Just to be rude about it, there were some really strange-looking books.

This is something that needs to be "played with," using a mock up of a few pages. Looking at a piece of paper on your desk doesn't do it. It needs to be in the context of the book binding to give a true visual effect. This book you are reading, just for reference, has an "inside" margin, which means the left margin for the right pages and the right margin for the left pages, of 0.9 inches. The "outside" margins are 0.7 inches.

MS Word, and I suspect other modern word processors, can do "mirror image" margins like this automatically, so you can make the inside margin a tad wider than the outside margin. The inside margin, next to the binding, naturally needs to be wide enough so you can comfortably read the text without prying open the pages. In addition, if your book is to be "perfect" bound, as this one is, the bindery will grind about a sixteenth of an inch off the back edge of the book in the process of gluing on the cover. If you choose the plastic "finger" or "coil" bindings that will lay open on the table, forget what I just said.

The outer margins for this book are 0.7 inches, just because I liked the way it looked. But you might think it looks a bit cramped on the edge, or maybe a little wasteful of paper, and would choose to move it in or out. Fair enough. Your eye may see things differently than mine and rightly so.

The top and bottom margins are both 1.0 inches on the pages you're reading. It leaves enough room for the page numbers to be easily read at the bottom and for headers at the top. Again, feel free to try something else and see how it looks to your critical eye. I forgot to mention that I wear trifocals.

Main text font—Now we're coming to the fun part. You get to play with fonts. This was always the best time for me, since my computer is loaded with fonts[3]. Fonts, like margins, need to be tested out in their true surroundings. This means you need to build up "practice" books to see what the text is really going to look like on the page. The "how-to" is in the next chapter.

In addition to trying out fonts to find the one that really turns you on, you need to fiddle with the size of the type. In this book the main text is printed in Times New Roman, 12 pt. How common! But I like it because it's clean and smooth and easy to read.

My first book used Bookman Old Style, 11 pt, which looks like this.

It has more "character" and isn't quite as compact as TNR, but I liked it at the time and still do.

When I was doing the final tune-up on my TI book, I spent a lot of time on fonts and sizes. I got into the "Font" function in the "Format" tool of MS Word and went crazy with all the stuff you can do. I ended up using an 11.5 point size and changing both the line spacing a tad because I thought it looked a little crowded on the page, and opening up the spacing between the letters just a hair. You can do absolutely anything with fonts in the word processors. By the way, if you're doing your book with a typewriter or a pencil, you may not want to spend a lot of time in this section. However, I seem to remember that the IBM Selectric typewriter has a changeable type ball.

While speaking of fonts, the subject of "justifying" the lines of type should be mentioned. For those of you not familiar with the term, this paragraph you're now reading is "left justified," which means that the left edge of the text, with exception of the paragraph indent, is smooth and even, and the right side is ragged because of the variable length of the lines of text. This is the style used throughout the book.

However, at the flip of a switch, metaphorically speaking, the word processors can justify your text on both the left side and the right side at the

---

[3] Not like my daughter Bev—she has 1000+ fonts in her computer. She's an artist and has an excuse. I don't. I just like fonts.

same time. This makes both edges of the text smooth at the expense of stretching the word spacings on the short lines to match the designated line length. This paragraph is an example of text that has been both right and left justified. It's strictly a personal choice. I prefer to leave the right side "as is" because I think it's easier to read if the words are all spaced the same. But it does look neat.

And of course, if you really want to freak people out, use right justified text. Why anyone would want to do this, except for advertising copy or special text placement, I don't know. But in the interests of illustrating all three types of "justification" I must include it. What I didn't illustrate is the "centered text" ability of word processors. This is what you use for headings and titles and such, in case you didn't already know.

Heading fonts—Same deal as the main text. You need to find a nice font—maybe one that's contrasting—for the chapter headings, the titles of the pages in the front matter and things of that sort. Or just use a larger size of your text font, and perhaps make it boldface or italic or both.

I liked the idea of using an all-caps font for the headings to give some contrast with the rest of the print. Another contrast would be a sans-serif style, like Century Gothic.

I LIKE COPPERPLATE GOTHIC LIGHT.

And I also like Century Gothic.

But I used Tempus Sans ITC for the headings in this book

Ah! So many fonts and so little time…

Page numbers—Books need page numbers for lots of reasons. Take your choice for the position on the page. I've gotten in the habit (three lousy books and I've got a habit?) of putting it centered at the bottom of the page, but MS Word gives you a "number" of options. (Sorry.)

Headers and footers—I'm not sure what you would use a footer for, but be my guest if you have the urge. Headers, however, I've used. They can carry the chapter number and title along with each page, or maybe the title of the book on the left-page header and the chapter information on the right-hand page.

I got creative in my TI book and added the year that the action was occurring on the top of each page in the header area. Good grief, *that* was a lot of trouble. MS Word and I went to Fist City before I was finished. But after all the pain and struggle, I liked it a lot. I think it adds to the book since the pages cover a 39-year time period.

Fancy stuff—I've seen some neat stuff in books that I liked but didn't have the nerve to try, like little decorative curlicues at the beginning and end of chapters, or on the title page. But it's easy to use the MS Word feature of a "dropped cap" for the first letter of the first word of each chapter. I think that looks cool. It's under "Format" as "Dropped Caps" Have fun.

And then there are those of you who don't care to fiddle with all the variables of book making. Simple and effective advice—find a book you like and copy it. You don't have to reinvent the wheel if you're content to hike the road already traveled. You've got plenty of company.

That's all I can think of to help you make your book a thing of beauty. But what *is* beauty? Very simply, it's a lack of ugly. A book that's thoughtfully formatted and crafted is beautiful because its form and style blend into a smooth background that doesn't offend the eye, and it lets the reader enjoy the content of the book without distraction or annoyance.

Chapter 9 – practice makes more perfect

As I promised, I'll show you how to make little "practice" books so you can see how all these neat ideas look in their own special world, like between two covers.

Decide on paper size, margins, fonts and whatever for your first try, so you can print out at least two pages of your text. Speaking of MS Word 97, to do a page size other than a full sheet of paper, you need to go to "File" and then to "Page Setup."

For example, if you want to see what 6 by 9 inch paper would look like in your practice book, with 1-inch margins all around, set the "Page Size" at 8.5 inches wide and 9.0 inches high, but use 8½ by 11 paper in your printer. Imagine, with a dotted line, where the edges would need to be trimmed to make the page 6 by 9 inches. Take a look at the sketch.

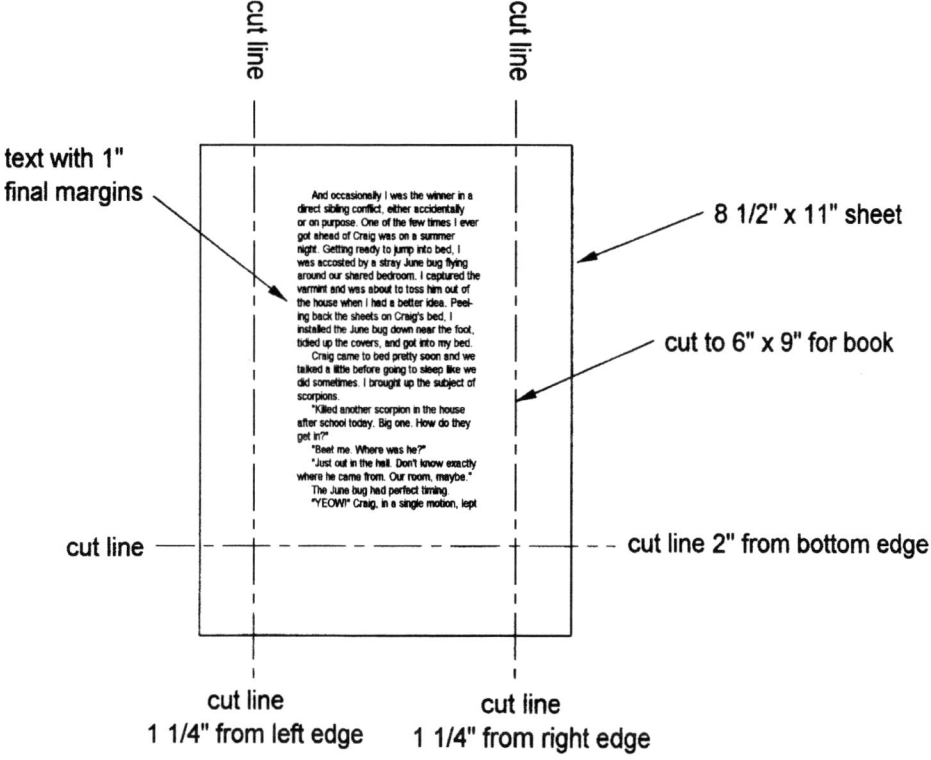

The answer is that you need to trim 1¼ inches from both sides of your piece of 8½ by 11 paper to make it 6 inches wide. For margins of 1 inch on both sides, set the margins in the Page Setup to 1¼ plus 1 equals 2¼ inches on each side. This, of course, lets you print on regular paper and do the trimming to size later. Also, if you have a printer that will print automatically on both sides of the page like my HP 970Cxi, the text will be centered on both sides instead of left justified which won't work. That takes care of the right and left sides.

The bottom margin doesn't need to be faked, since the printer is already fooled into thinking it's printing your book on 8½ by 9-inch paper. You've decided on a 1-inch bottom margin also, so just set your bottom margin to 1 inch. Of course, after printing you're going to have to trim 2 inches of paper from the bottom edge to make the paper 9 inches tall.

Your top margin doesn't have to be adjusted, since the top of the page is the only edge you're not going to screw up with a pair of scissors. Set your top margin for 1 inch, and then print two practice pages that are full of text—a left page and a right page with the even page number smaller than the odd, like pages 4 and 5, or 88 and 89. Trust me. Put the two pages together with the printing face-to-face and square them up neatly. Actually, I usually print eight or ten pages, (four or five sheets of paper) in which case I generally start on any odd-numbered page, a right-hand page, because my printer can print both sides of the sheets automatically.

After a little practice, you might want to add two pieces of something like "medium card stock" (67# Wassau Exact Bristol, for example) to the outsides of your two or more pages to use as simulated covers. It'll make it open more like a book. Place the stack face up on your trimmer.

Using the trimming board's scale, cut 1¼ inches off the right side of these pages. Then rotate them a quarter turn counterclockwise and cut 2 inches off the bottom. Rotate it another quarter turn and trim the final 1¼ from what should be the left edge of your stack. With any luck at all you will have 6 x 9 pages with your text neatly centered on them.

I'm not just being fussy about what edge to cut first and how to rotate the paper between cuts. To make the pages be the same shape, especially if you're actually making a real book and having to cut your pages in small groups because of the trimmer capacity, do them all the same way. They may not be exactly square but they'll be the same shape and match up in a stack. If you don't have a trimming board, just do it carefully with the scissors and you can achieve a perfectly satisfactory sample book. But you have to stick your tongue out of the corner of your mouth while you're cutting.

Check the text inside to be sure where the "binding" should go, and mark a line with a pencil along the left side of the "cover" (or the top piece of paper) ¼ inch from the edge. With a regular office or home stapler, carefully staple this "book" in three places—the center and an inch and a half in from both the top and bottom. It should look something like this:

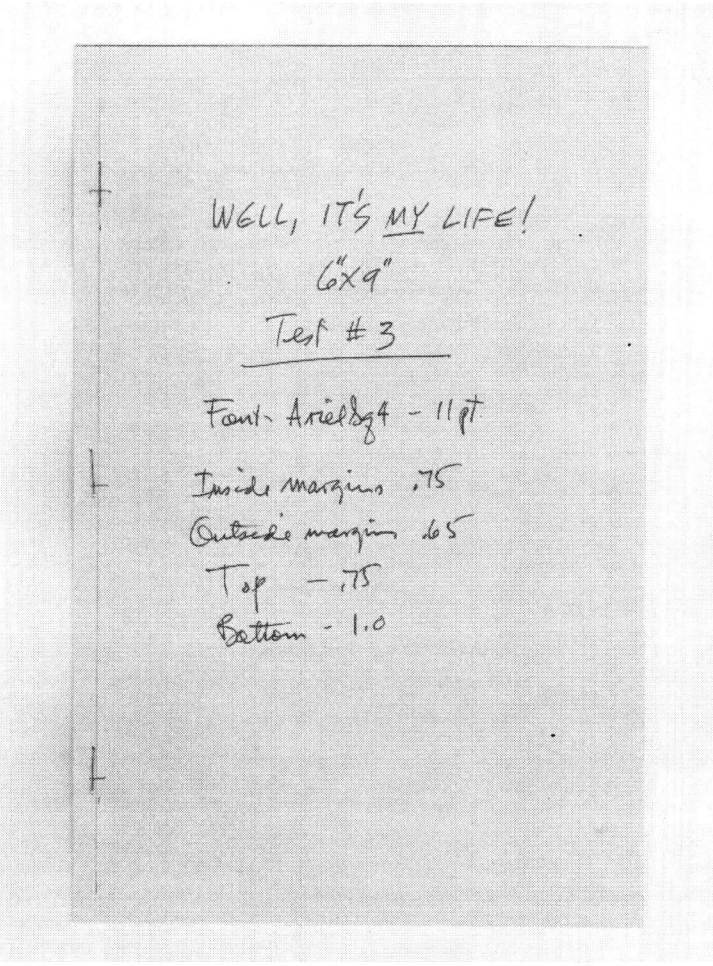

You've now made a "book," which has all the features, except thickness, that your finished book would have if it were built to the same specifications. Later, you may find it advantageous to print a dozen pages and build a little bigger fake book to get a better feel of it. But in any case, you have something you can stand back from and admire, and decide if you like it. Does the size feel right? Do you like the font? Is the size of the printing okay? Is it easy to read? Do the margins look strange? Are the page numbers and headers where they belong?

Once again, compare it with a "real" book if you're not sure. Begin to look at other books, and now your own, with the eye of an artist—a writer *and* an artist. You've put a lot of effort into this book, so it deserves to look great.

You say the type looks too large? Like a big-print or a children's book? Good eye. Change your font size down a point, or two, or maybe just a fraction of a point. It can be done in Word under "Format" and then "Font." Print and staple up another set of pages. Compare the two. Try something else. Make the page larger and fiddle with the margins...

You get the idea. If *anything* bothers your eye or your finer sensibilities, fix it. It's easy to do with the little minibooks, and the final result will be a handsome book. It will be a handsome book because you put the appropriate effort into making it handsome, and because you saw what it was going to look like, *exactly* like, before you spent your money and had it printed and bound. Good work!

Chapter 10 – do the cover

I've saved the discussion of the cover until last for a very good reason: I don't know what to tell you. The amount of effort and money you can spend on a book cover can vary from nothing to a lot and anywhere in between. For example, if you've decided to take the plunge and go for a hardback binding, about all you have to do is tell the bindery what the name of the book is, and your name, and they'll put that on the spine, generally at no charge. For extra money they'll put it on the cover, too. Your big decision might be what color you want it printed or hot-stamped in. Nothing to it.

The first printing of my childhood book, which was done the "old-fashioned way" by a non-digital printing company, cost a *ton*, and the additional cost of a hard binding didn't seem too bad in comparison. Also, when I was doing my first book, money didn't seem as important, but I've gotten over *that*, thank heavens.

My suggestion is for you to call a bindery and ask questions. There are options for hardback covers that I didn't mention, and more, I'm sure, that I don't know about.

The other extreme is to design a paperback cover for your little darling. This can be a simple piece of art or it can run into a lot of work or a lot of money. The wonderful paper cover on my TI book was done using Adobe Photoshop by my daughter Bev the Artist, the one with all the fonts. And it's a terrific cover because she's really good at it. I gave it to the digital printing company on a CD-ROM in a "psd" format, which they liked.

After discussing the digital printing company's requirements and passing the information along to Bev, she laid out the cover full-sized, to be centered and printed sideways on an 11 x 17 sheet of paper. The final size of the printed cover is that of a piece of paper that wraps completely around three sides of the book, and forms a new front, back and spine. It's also just a bit—like ⅛-inch—wider on three sides than the actual book pages so that it can be trimmed to exact size after binding.

As your Little-Known Fact for the Day, not too many years ago the British printing houses printed the lengthwise spine writing on thin books so that it was upside-down if a book were lying face up on a table. I noticed when I was scanning a shelf of books at a used book store that every now and then I would have to stop twisting my head to the right to read the spines, and twist it to the left. And it would be an older British-printed book. I have no idea what the reasoning for this was, but I'm sure it was the result of quite a discussion back in the sixteenth century or such time.

The spine part of the cover artwork should have the name of your book along with writer's name, which is you, and usually it's just the last name. And it should be right side up when the book is face up on the table.

As a Child in the MacGregor Clan ----Drummond

Of course, if you write a 600-pager, then the spine will be fat enough for you to put anything your heart desires on it, and standing up besides.

As a Child in the MacGregor Clan   or   Life Among the Savages   by   Gavine Drummond Earl of Perth

The layout of the cover "wrap" needs to accurately take into account the thickness of the book so that the spine section will be the proper width, and it will wrap properly around the stack of pages. I spent some time with a pair of dial calipers and piles of paper to be sure I gave Bev the right thickness dimension. Everyone else can just ask the printing-person how wide the spine will be. They have cheat-sheets with the types of paper and the number of pages. But I believe I already mentioned I'm an engineer and I prefer to do my own numbers if I can. I don't mind getting involved in all aspects of the book business.

But you don't have to use Photoshop or one of the fancier art programs. A cover, spine, and back can be just text and you could do it yourself with MS Word or other word processor program. I would think that Word 97 has the capabilities, since you can obviously turn text sideways (see above) and do other cute things with it. I don't have the knowledge or courage to try, but it might be worth a shot. As usual, talk to your printer first about the suitability of their equipment to use your output files.

If you feel inadequate, as I did, but have no assistant to fall back on, your printing company can generally design a cover for a sum. You just give them your sketches and ideas and money. And if you don't like it, give them more sketches and more money.

I'll give you some free and unsolicited advice at this point: go a little overboard on the cover. You've paid your dues and then some in the writing and formatting of this production, so don't shortchange it with a weenie cover. Spend some time and money on it if you have to, or better yet, browbeat a talented sibling, or child (as I did), or grandchild or friend into helping you with it. Don't wrap your silk purse in a sow's ear. Wrap it in a silk ear that you can be proud of.

This is not to say that your cover needs to be incredibly fancy and colorful to be a success. On the contrary, a well-done one-color cover can be quite effective. The key words here are "well-done." Color can certainly be used to wonderful effect on the jacket, but colors add cost. Adding thoughtfulness to the design is cheaper.

One last complication. Should you spring for the ISBN (International Standard Book Number) and matching UPC (Universal Product Code) bar code for your book or not? It's expensive and may not be necessary. If you plan to actively sell your book, I'd recommend doing it. Having the ISBN and bar code on the back jacket makes it a real book, commerce-wise. If, however, like most of us, you sell a few and give away the rest, it's not necessary. But if you can interest Barnes and Noble in your work, you're going to need an ISBN. It depends on your optimism. By the way, shop around for it. Prices vary.

Going with the ISBN means that you have to integrate the UPC bar code and ISBN in a box on your back cover. I purchased mine through the printing company and the ISBN and UPC came to me in the form of a Photoshop file, a dot psd. It then has to be put into the back cover art in the appropriate place. No big deal, but it's some extra work on the cover art.

Like everything else, you really need to talk to a printer or printers before rushing off and doing your cover. They have their own specialties and limitations, and talk is cheap if done earlier rather than later. The next chapter is about getting your book printed, and it includes talking to your prospective printing person, and what questions to ask.

Chapter 11 – getting it printed

You have finally finished your book. Now it's time to get it printed, bound, and sprung on the unsuspecting world, or at least on your family. There are many possibilities, depending on how you wrote your book and how you want the final product to look. Since this is an increasingly high-tech world, let's start with the highest-tech approach, which also gives a highly satisfactory product at a reasonable cost. This approach is to take your book, in "virtual" digital format, to a "digital press," and let them print your book pages and your cover, and assemble them with a method called a "perfect" binding. You will have a paperback book with a slick, color jacket. I didn't say we were trying to save money—spring for the color jacket. You'll like it.

But before you take your book and artwork on a CD-ROM or diskettes to the digital press, you need to meet them and ask questions. I have not done an extensive survey of the digital printing equipment that is being used, but whatever your chosen printer has will determine certain requirements for your incoming book data. Here are a few of the possible questions and answers:

- Q: Can I bring you my book in a "dot doc" file from Microsoft Word?

  A: Well, I guess so. If you just *have* to…

- Q: What formats do you prefer?

  A: Adobe PageMaker is good for the PC, and QuarkXPress on the Mac.

- Q: How about my cover art? Can you handle Photoshop "dot psd" files?"

  A: Yes. Adobe's Photoshop is good, and so is their Illustrator.

- Q: I've got some neat fonts in my text. Any problem with *HooplaSans*?

  A: Well, er… good grief. Let me have a list of them and I'll check. You may have to supply a file of the font if I can't support it.

- Q: How should I do my Word "Page Setup" [under 'File'] to fit your printing machinery?

  A: Since you want a 6 x 9 finished page size, choose [   ] for your paper size, and justify your text [   ]. This way, I can [   ], which will save you some money. But you need to [   ] to your format to take into account the [   ]. (Fill in the blanks. Printers are different.)

- Q: How can your machine print both sides of the page and make them line up if the text isn't centered?

  A: It just can.

- Q: What kind of paper should I use for the book?

  A: Regular good-quality 20# bond will work, but for a slight additional cost I can print in on 60# offset paper, which is about like 24# bond. The printing on the back doesn't show through as much and it looks and feels better. However, if you're a cheap bastard, we can go with the 20#.

- Q: What kind of paper would you suggest for the cover?

  A: The cover can be printed in black or in color on C1S 10 point paper, which means "coated one side," 110# stock. That's pretty standard for paperbacks, but some people use C1S 8 point, which, at 80#, is a little lighter.

- Q: What's it going to cost?

  A: I need to know the paper you want to use and the size of the book, the number of colors on the cover, and how many copies you want printed. And if the computer files you give me are not "print ready," then I'll have to charge you to get them arranged properly. Also, if you want an ISBN, I can take care of that and supply you with the artwork file for it, but you'll have to add it to your cover art or pay me to. When I know all those things, I can give you a quotation.

- Q: To finish my cover artwork, I need to know the exact thickness of the book so I can figure the wrap around the spine. Can you tell me?

  A: I need to know the weight of the paper we're going to use and how many pages total, and then I can tell you. You first...

- Q: Do you have a restroom I can use?

  A: Sure. Down the hall on the right.

That's pretty much the way my conversation went when we sat down to talk. And just for your information, the digital press that printed my first digital book, the TI one, also printed this one. I now understand their needs and they understand mine, and their prices are competitive. We get along just fine.

I recently visited three more printer/binderies and talked to them about short-run self-published books. It was easy to tell who had dealt with the self-publishing authors—they would accept MS Word, albeit somewhat grudgingly. It's not what "professional" people use, but it's sure what everybody else uses, like you and me.

One very nice printing shop convinced me that it would be to my advantage to bring them my book printed one page to a sheet, on "28# laser copy paper" instead of on a CD-ROM in the Word format. They would print my book on their high-speed copiers, and I'm sure it would look just fine.

If your most convenient printing company has serious Fear of Word, this might be the best way to get your book printed. It's a true WYSIWYG (What You See Is What You Get) which makes it your fault if the book is screwed up. It's probably the only way you could get a page printed upside-down, for example. Incidentally, another print shop with a high-speed copier said to bring the originals on 20# or 24# bond, because 28# bond wouldn't feed properly in their machine. Ask.

Dealing in the digital format has some advantages that a stack of paper doesn't, and remains my first choice. A particular printer's handout of "Artwork Submission Guidelines" lists only Mac format files for their "preferred" types. However, with their "cross-platform capabilities" (great phrase) they can accept Windows/PC files in five formats, with Word and its kin being the last choice. Nice people and a nice shop, but not accustomed to dealing with us amateur writers.

Now you've found a great printer who can do a turnkey job—printing, cover, and perfect binding. You make a few decisions, fix your files to fit the printer's requirements and you're ready to go in the book business. Take your freshly-burned CD-ROM back to the printer, sign your contract, and write a check for half the total. Then, go home and sit by your telephone.

"Newbie Writer? Your books are ready…" *Hot damn!*

Other ways to make books

There are several options besides the do-everything digital printing company and bindery. Let's break down the process of making a book into the two main activities—printing the pages and binding them. First let's look at ways of printing the pages, with the pros and cons of each.

Do-It-Yourself printing

The cheapest and in some cases the quickest way to print a small number of books (if they're not too big) is to print them yourself. I have an ink-jet printer, a relatively modern Hewlett Packard 970Cxi, that is able to print both sides of a sheet automatically. Not very fast, but time is cheap around the house. I printed 11 copies of one edition of my 175-page TI book, in the 8½ x 11 format, on my printer, one after another, with no noticeable ill effects. This, along with homegrown bindings, allowed me to meet a Christmas deadline.

That's a lot of pages for a home printer, and it takes a lot of ink cartridges to feed it. I could get about five 175-page books out of a $25 black cartridge. My local chain office-type printery will do double-sided printing for $.14/sheeet, or .07/printed side in small quantities. This drops to $.03/side in huge quantities. So at my house that's about $.03/page for ink plus less than $.01 for paper, disregarding wear and tear on the equipment, versus probably $.05 for those who have to make a profit. Pretty close.

If you don't have an automatic two-sided printer, follow the instructions for printing one side and then reloading the stack and printing the other side. Most word processor and printers support this sort of thing. If you have the nerve, and I did lots of times, you can load up your printer with fresh paper, turn it on to print your book, and go to bed. In the morning, with any luck, you'll have another copy of your book.

But you don't want an 8 ½ x 11 book? Understandable. So, using the setup from the chapter on making the minibooks, print your entire book in whatever smaller format you desire, and as before, centered from left to right and top-justified on 8 ½ x 11 pages. You can let the bindery take care of trimming.

This Do-It-Yourself printing has two main advantages over the usual copy-shop Xerox copying which is next on our list. If your computer printer is capable of color printing, and certainly all the newer ink jet printers are, you can print your book with color pictures. This, of course, assumes that you scanned in your photos in color. Second, the quality of your home printer is better than the

Xerox copiers in general. The printing is crisper and the uniformity better. You might consider printing a few copies in color and having them professionally bound as "Special Editions" for family members or as gifts.

High-speed copier printing

The high-speed copier has its plusses and minuses. The plusses are that it's high-speed and that it copies. But it doesn't do as well on pictures. If your book has a lot of neat photos and pictures, you might want to spend more money and go with digital printing. The same preparation of originals for high-speed copier printing applies to the digital "scanning" method of digital printing. But if your book is mostly text, or you don't mind the picture of Uncle Herman's hand-carved totem pole being a little muddy, stick with the copier.

As I mentioned earlier, if you want someone to print your book on a high-speed copier, you must supply them with a set of originals from which to print, preferably on good quality paper of a type and weight the printer recommends. Whatever method you used to originally write your book, be it computer with printer, typewriter, pen and ink, or No. 2 yellow pencil, you need to pull together a complete set of finished pages, preferably one *page* to a *sheet* of paper, like only on the front. If it's not too late, use the paper the printer recommends. And if you're printing up a set from your computer, for Pete's sake, don't use the your printer's *draft* mode. Print it *pretty*, because this will be the master copy they print your book from. In addition, it needs to feed reliably in their machine. Listen to their recommendations on paper. It doesn't happen very often, but if a page gets wadded-up while being fed at 90 mph through the monster copying machine, it'll take awhile to put Humpty-Dumpty back together again.

This stack of papers that will turn into copies of your book must have a copy of *every page* in your book on the front of a *separate sheet*, including blank ones. The magic high-speed copiers will automatically pick up the first sheet in your stack and print it as the first page, the right-hand page, of your book. For example, this might be your title page. So the first page in your stack must be an odd numbered page, like "i" or "1." When the machine has printed that page on its first piece of paper, it turns it over and prints your second page on the back. Like this would be your "ii" or "2." Your third page becomes the front of the second printed sheet, your fourth the back of the second sheet, and so forth. Only it does it so fast you have no idea what it's doing. It doesn't know what it's doing either, so it would behoove you to *get your pages in the right order*. Especially check to be sure you have a blank *sheet* in your master stack for every blank *page* in your book.

What! You wrote your book on *both* sides of the paper? You're in luck, because the copiers can also automatically print up an exact copy of a stack of papers. It just doesn't do it as fast or with the same precision, and you might get a little copy bleed-through from the back, but it can be done. So put your pages in order, just like you want the book, and start looking for a printer. But *next* time just write on the front.

Shop around in your cruising radius and talk to the printers about running your book copies for you. Don't forget to specify the type of paper you want them printed on. It might be worth a few bucks to have a shop print up a few pages of your book using the paper you decided on, especially pages with pictures, and compare them with samples from other printers.

The digital press

If you want the best quality printing for your book, find a digital press that will print your book solely on their digital xerographic printing equipment. The cost goes up, and so does the quality. It's like printing it yourself at home, only with a lot less effort. The digitally printed output that I've seen is noticeably better the high-speed copier. Photos, for example, are printed at 600 dpi, or dots per inch.

The input for the digital printing equipment can either be digital files on a CD-ROM or diskette, or a stack of printed originals as discussed in the high-speed copier section. The printer can print directly from a digital file or it can scan originals and print from them. Clever machine. The output in either case is excellent, and if photos and pictures are your bag, go with it, either way.

One other point in favor of xerographic printing, either digital or copier, is that the long-term stability of inkjet printing may be inferior to the Xerox process printing. Even when printed on acid-free paper, which most of the modern bond papers are, inkjet ink can change chemically and possibly fade with time. It would be a hell of a note if your hard-fought book turned into a set of blank pages, like the old joke book, *What Men Know about Women*. It might be wise to print a few books with different technologies, just to be sure.

And that completes the printing of your book. So how do we fasten the pages together to make it easier to read? Next chapter.

Chapter 12 – getting it bound

The cost of binding your printed pages can vary from practically nothing to a lot, and the resulting book will range from perfectly adequate for reading to a beautiful work of art. I've tried them all. My personal favorite is the paperback "perfect" binding, which is middle of the road. Like the most bang for the buck, to use an old cliché. But nothing says you have to bind all your copies the same way—some can get a functional binding and maybe a few the deluxe treatment.

Hard-back binding

If you are Mr. or Mrs. Moneybags, track down an old-fashioned bindery and have them hand-bind your books for you. They will be gorgeous, complete with hot-stamped gold lettering on the front and the spine, with durable and bulletproof covers, and the pages sewn in place forever. Like they'll never fall out. The books will be beautiful beyond belief. It can truly be an art form. But the down side, as you have suspected all along, is that it's quite expensive because of the hand labor. But still, keep it in mind if you want a few special copies, because they will really be special.

But wait, there's hope. There are a few hard-back binderies that are quite reasonable. One that I've used is The Library Binding Company in Waco, Texas. They specialize in rebinding school textbooks and have mastered the process of sewn-spine hard cover binding in a cost-effective way. Not sewn "signatures," mind you, since that's a different horse, but the spine is stitched before gluing, forming a very professional-looking and durable book. The standard jacket material is buckram, and is available in a dozen or fifteen colors. Printing the title and author's name on the spine is included in the very reasonable price. This good news is augmented by the pleasant surprise of no minimum quantity. At this time, hard binding one to ten copies of a medium-sized book costs $10.00 each. Over ten and the price drops to $7.95.

Paperback "perfect" binding

This type of binding, which is basically done by roughing-up and gluing the spine of your pages to a wrap-around cover, seems to be the *de facto* standard for self-publishing. Not too many years ago, a "perfect-bound" book was anything but—if the pages didn't fall out by the second reading, it was a "wonder" book.

But improvements have been made, and today's perfect bindings are quite satisfactory, and have the added advantage of allowing a decorative and informative cover to introduce your book without the added hassle of a dust jacket. They look nice, and the process is reasonably priced.

One limitation is for thin books—the perfect binding doesn't work well if the spine is much less than ¼-inch thick. This would be about 80 pages, or 40 sheets, more or less, of the 60# paper. Some printers have newer equipment and can bind thinner volumes. Again, if you have a thin book, ask.

However you printed your books, you can take the stacks of pages to a bindery and have them trimmed and perfect bound. But there's one catch—you've had to do your cover art and have it printed, probably on 11 x 17 C1S 10 point stock. Can't do a classy perfect binding without doing a cover. Unless, like me, you brought in two copies of a hand-Xeroxed "bootleg copy" of an out-of-print book I had sought for years to be trimmed and perfect bound. The bindery was nice enough to put the name on a plain white cover wrap, no charge. I was planning on a Marks-a-Lot.

But this gets back to the problem of who does what and to whom on your book. It's convenient to let a "digital press" do it all, if they can, including the cover and the binding. It's not so convenient to print it yourself, find someone to do color copies of your cover, and a third party to bind them. But it can be done, and just might be the cheapest way. There are lots of opportunities to be creative besides the writing part.

Plastic comb, coil, saddle-stitched, tape and other bindings

A really easy and quick way to get a book bound is to take it to the office-type printery and get a plastic comb or plastic coil binding put on it. They can usually do a few while you wait, and certainly for trial or experimental copies, it's a good way to do it. Some of you might even have the equipment to do this yourselves, left over from doing the church annual cookbook or something.

The down side is that your book, that you've worked so hard on, now *looks* like a cookbook. And there's no place to put the author's name on the spine. But it's cheap and durable, and will lie flat on the kitchen counter. Like a cookbook.

Investigate other types of bindings if hard back or perfect binding is not your cup of tea. Very thin books, like pamphlets or really uneventful childhoods, can be saddle-stitched. For all the fancy name, it looks a lot like someone stapled the pages through the middle and folded it in two. But it's fine for things without too many pages. One bindery suggested that something less than 90 pages could be bound this way. Again, it probably depends on the type of paper and the bindery.

Tape binding is an inexpensive method, and there are some proprietary methods, like "FAS binding." Poke around your neighborhood and see what the shops have to offer.

Do-It-Yourself bindings

You didn't think I was going to suggest a homemade binding for your books, did you? You were wrong. There is a place for such a rough-and-ready binding, and I've done a lot of them. Believe it or not, when I was "finishing" my TI book, I printed and hand-bound a total of 22 copies in various versions. I wanted certain people to see it before I really turned it loose, and it was a convenient way of doing it.

The other use I've found was for binding small, personal writings that I'd done and wanted to share with my friends and family, whether they liked it or not. Do you like science fiction? Let me know and I'll send you some…

You now have, for example, ten copies of your book printed and stacked in a crisscross pile on your table. It's time to make your DIY cover. Disregard everything I've said about covers, and just bring up a clean page on your computer screen and generate a nice cover, using all those swell fonts you've been admiring. Or cheat and copy your title page and doll it up a bit. It would be well to move your cover "art" a little to the right on the page, because the tape binding on the spine offsets the open space of the cover. You'll see what I mean when you finish the first one and the cover looks lopsided.

I suggest that you print your cover on card stock, readily available in many colors, like I discussed for the mini-practice books. My printer will handle the 67# "medium card stock" with no problems. I've also used 110# "heavy card stock, smooth finish" which looks nice, but my printer can only feed one at a time when it's this heavy. Print ten copies of your cover. If you're of such a mind, feed it back through your printer and print something else on the inside, like who you are and when they were printed. Or make up a funny name for your "printing company" to disguise the fact that you're not spending any money on the book. Ever heard of "the little print shop on forestridge?" Guess who.

Restack each set of book pages with a cover on the front and a matching blank sheet of card stock on the back. All that's left to do now is the world's cheapest binding. And for that, you need a stapler. Actually, you need a ***STAPLER***. A regular weenie office stapler isn't going to cut it for this. You need a heavy-duty stapler and special staples. Mine, from one of the chain office-supply stores, is a Swingline Model 390, which claims to be a "160-sheet stapler." That is some serious stapling, like for a 320-page book, using ¾-inch staples. But unless you can round up King Kong to help, I'd advise keeping this type of pseudo-binding under 200 pages, which can probably use the ½-inch staples. I'm sure there are other brands and models of staplers that can also do this job. Mine was under $30, which seemed a bargain.

Set the depth guide on the stapler, if it has one, to ¼-inch, otherwise draw a pencil line ¼-inch from the left-hand edge of your cover, from top to bottom. Then put a cross mark in the center of this line, like at 5 ½-inches from the ends. Two more marks at 1 ¾-inches from each end, and you're ready to try out your new big honking stapler.

By the way, I might suggest practicing first on a thick stack of scrap paper, since these super-mondo staplers require a little finesse in their operation. You should have enough used 20# bond in your wastebasket by now to make another book, if not the *Encyclopedia Britannica*, so jog up a bunch and practice stapling.

When your confidence level changes from negative to positive, give your first book a try. Don't forget to "jog" the stack neatly, preferably against the outside edges, the right side, of your book and not the left. The right's the side you can see and it needs to be neat and tidy.

I had trouble at first stapling a thick stack and keeping the pages lined up. I solved this problem by using four big, strong spring paper clamps that I carefully put on the stack after jogging. These are big suckers, and take a lot of squeeze to open them, but they keep the paper in position during the stapling very nicely. I put one on the top edge, one on the bottom edge, and two on the right side. Leave the side to be stapled clear. The paper wouldn't dare move.

Do the three staples, beginning with the center one. Take the spring clamps off and admire the bundle of pages. You've nearly finished your first book. I do a little smoothing on the staple points with a small hammer and a block. Put the front of your book facedown on the block and gently tap the sharp ends of the staples down flat onto the paper.

I forgot to tell you that you need to go to the hardware store for the finishing touch. Sorry. Get one or more rolls of 1½-inch-wide vinyl tape. I've found a 3M product called Scotch Plastic tape, cleverly enough, that comes in four or five colors to match or contrast with your card stock covers. You're going to fold a strip of this over the spine of your book to cover the staples and make it look finished.

Figure out how far from the edge the tape should start on the front cover by measuring the thickness of your book, subtracting that from 1½ and dividing the result by two. I suggest you make a couple of light pencil marks a bit less than the proper distance and overlap the tape slightly when you put it on so the marks don't show. What could be easier?

Just cut off a piece of tape about a foot long, and carefully stick it down on the front cover, guided by your pencil marks. Smooth it down on the front, then fold it over and smooth it on the spine, and then smooth it onto the back cover. It doesn't make any difference if it laps a little different on the front and back. Take scissors and trim the excess tape from the top and bottom of the spine, and you're finished. With one book, anyhow.

I will confess that I've become addicted to writing, and have been writing practically non-stop since I found out how much fun it was. In the process, I've printed and bound dozens of books by this method, both 8 ½ x 11 and 6 x 9. The smaller ones take hours hunched over a paper cutter, cutting five sheets at a time, but it can be done. Ask my friends who have to read them.

Chapter 13 – Well, *now* what?

Well, now what, indeed? You've paid out of your own pocket to have 20 copies of your book printed and bound, and they're sitting on the floor of your den in a cardboard box. You must have given some thought about who would like to have a copy of it, like everybody in your family, reading age or not, and a few friends that you've talked to about it. They said they'd like to see it when you were finished.

So finally, after all the blood, sweat and tears, midnight oil, hard-earned dollars, and a few other clichés, it's time to eat a little dessert. It's *fun* to give away your books. You're proud of it, and rightly so, and now you can share it with others.

I would recommend that you keep a list of the people you give copies to, because in a few months you won't be able to remember whether you sent one to Aunt Matilda or not. Or is that just me? Write it down. I think you'll be surprised at the number of people who would like to read your book. A personal story of growing up, or service in the military, or a career can be keenly interesting to people who know you.

I remember how I felt when I heard that Harry Waugh, the activator of my writing addiction, had written a book of his growing up in Louisiana. I've known Harry since the early 1950's, and know his family and had met his parents and visited them in Louisiana. But I knew almost nothing of Harry's young life or about life in Louisiana at the same time I was growing up in Texas. I was interested. I was really interested in reading about Harry's early years. It would be a new look at an old friend.

On a different plane, I was interested that Harry had written a book. All by himself. This I had to see. And I think you'll have friends and acquaintances who will feel the same way. You will be unique in your circle because *you have written a book*. They will be curious about your story, and they'll be curious about why and how you wrote it.

Face it, my friend, you're in the tiny minority of people who actually sat down and wrote a book. Many talk of it but few do it. You're practically famous. So be prepared to pass out more copies of your new baby than you figured. Maybe you should have printed 50 copies.

And then there's the awkward question—to sell or not to sell? I'm a poor person to give advice on this subject. It was embarrassing to ask someone to pay real money for a copy of my book. Who did I think I was, Stephen King? But I got over it when someone actually bought a book. It's still more fun to give them away, but selling a few helps pay the bills.

In case you were trying to decide what I was recommending, don't bother. I really don't have any good advice on this subject. What I did, eventually, was to give copies to my nearest and dearest, both family and friends, but others, out beyond some magic boundary of friendship, were given a price when they asked about the book.

If your book has some general interest outside of your family and friends, set yourself up to sell it and give it a shot. This is certainly true if your book has genealogical appeal, namely family connections. Lots, if not most, of the books in the genealogical field, primarily family histories, are sold. It's just part of the genealogy territory. Being paid for this type of book encourages authors to write and make family histories available by defraying some of the cost.

If you sell a book in Texas, you're expected to have a tax permit, collect the sales tax, and send it to the State of Texas. Most other states have similar statutes. So there's another reason to give books away. It's less paperwork. But if you've written the book with the idea of recouping some of the printing and binding costs by selling it, do it right. It's not really that big a deal. Here's the simplest way to become an official bookseller and tax collector in Texas:

1. Register an "assumed name," which sounds strangely illegal, but it's just the legal term for a DBA, a "Doing Business As" name. This is done through your County Clerk's office in Texas. You are speaking to Ed Millis, proprietor of Ed Millis Books, registered as such in Dallas County and selling books in Texas.

2. Apply to the Comptroller of Public Accounts for a Texas Sales and Use Tax Permit. This document will allow you (and require you) to collect the state tax on any in-state sales of your book. Mail order sales outside of Texas do not require the tax to be paid.

You should do these two relatively easy exercises if you're serious about selling your books. And of course, waving your new tax permit in front of the printer/bindery cash register will waive your sales tax when you pay for your books. You're not avoiding the taxes; you're just postponing them and passing them on to the final purchaser of your book. Be *sure* you understand the rules about buying books without paying the state sales tax and then giving them away. And, naturally, selling books and collecting taxes means you must keep track of all sales and periodically do an accounting and send the taxes to the state where they belong.

But what's that you say? Your book is of worldwide interest and could be a best-selling smash hit? Then you should get it published instead of selling it yourself or giving it away. Think big! And maybe, think again. The publishing world is a cruel place and breaking into that world is difficult. Very difficult. But it can be done, and obviously is done with regularity. *Harry Potter* comes to mind. Give it a try if you feel that your book has good general or specific appeal. I guarantee that it will be an interesting experience.

There are two ways to get your book published. The first way is to get a literary agent to represent you in the book publishing world, and the second is to present your work directly to a publisher. I will fade out of this picture and leave you with the advice to visit your favorite bookstore, either real or virtual, and buy a copy of the latest *Writer's Market* or *Writer's Guide to Book Editors, Publishers and Literary Agents.* These books will tell you who, what, why, where, how, and more, about getting published. My absolute last piece of advice, as I finish my fading like the Cheshire cat, is to double-check the information in the books. Find the website of the company or person you're considering sending your manuscript to and get the latest information on what and how to submit. Good luck. You'll need it.

One final note about your new book. I'd love to read it and see what you've done. I'll make you a deal: send me a copy and I'll give you back every cent you paid for this little book, including tax and shipping. And don't forget, I have a list of everyone I gave free copies to, so no cheating.

And that, dear and patient reader, is my version of the art, science, and I hope, the mystery of writing your own book. I'll close by repeating my advice in the preface: *Do it!*

the end

Index